PENGUIN BOOKS
HOW TO BE A YANK

George Mikes was born in 1912 in Siklós, Hungary. He studied law and received his doctorate from Budapest University. He became a journalist and was sent to London as a correspondent to cover the Munich crisis. He came for a fortnight but stayed on and made England his home. During the Second World War he broadcast for the BBC Hungarian Service, where he remained until 1951. He continued working as a freelance broadcaster and writer until his death in 1987.

In 1946 he published *How to be an Alien*, which went into thirty editions and identified the author as a humorist writer, although he had not intended the book to be funny. *How to be a Yank* is made up of three of his earlier books, *How to Scrape Skies* (1948), *Wisdom for Others* (1950) and *Shakespeare and Myself* (1952). His other books include *Über Alles, Little Cabbages, Italy for Beginners, How to Unite Nations, How to be Inimitable, How to Tango, The Land of the Rising Yen, How to Run a Stately Home* (with the Duke of Bedford), *Switzerland for Beginners, How to be Decadent, Tsi-Tsa, English Humour for Beginners, How to be Poor, How to be a Guru, How to be a Brit* and *How to be God*. He wrote a study of the Hungarian Revolution and is also the author of *A Study of Infamy*, an analysis of the Hungarian secret political police system, *Arthur Koestler: The Story of a Friendship* and *The Riches of the Poor: A Journey round the World Health Organisation*. On his seventieth birthday, in 1982, he published his autobiography, *How to be Seventy*.

GEORGE MIKES

HOW TO BE
A YANK

and More Wisdom

Another Mikes Minibus
comprising

HOW TO SCRAPE SKIES
WISDOM FOR OTHERS
SHAKESPEARE AND MYSELF

Nicolas Bentley drew the pictures
for *How to Scrape Skies* and *Wisdom for Others*

David Langdon illustrated
Shakespeare and Myself

PENGUIN BOOKS

PENGUIN BOOKS

Published by the Penguin Group
27 Wrights Lane, London w8 5tz, England
Viking Penguin Inc., 40 West 23rd Street, New York, New York 10010, USA
Penguin Books Australia Ltd, Ringwood, Victoria, Australia
Penguin Books Canada Ltd, 2801 John Street, Markham, Ontario, Canada l3r 1b4
Penguin Books (NZ) Ltd, 182–190 Wairau Road, Auckland 10, New Zealand

Penguin Books Ltd, Registered Offices: Harmondsworth, Middlesex, England

This collection first published by André Deutsch 1987
Published in Penguin Books 1989
1 3 5 7 9 10 8 6 4 2

Reproduced, printed and bound in Great Britain by
Hazell Watson & Viney Limited
Member of BPCC plc
Aylesbury, Bucks, England

CONTENTS

PREFACE

The first of these three books was the result of a clever ploy. In 1946 my little book *How to be an Alien* proved to be quite a success. A few months later my mother went to America where my brother lived, and my sister was expected to follow her. I had not seen them since before the war (except for my mother, who paid me a short visit in London on her way to new York), and as – curiously enough – I love my family I was keen on joining them. It was my wife who came up with the simple but brilliant idea: 'Why don't you go over and write a sort of *How to be an Alien* book about the Americans?' These few words settled the problem of my journey, and they also settled my life style for the next twenty years or more: I was to continue travelling from country to country, writing books about them. *How to Scrape Skies* was very enjoyable to write. Having undertaken it because I loved my family, I found that I loved the Americans too – and also found them even stranger than my family, which was saying a good deal.

Wisdom for Others contains my wise views about life. I have always had a passion for giving unsolicited advice to all and sundry. As I wrote in a much later book, *How to be a Guru*, 'I am a very wise man. Not terribly intelligent, highly educated or brilliantly clever, but very wise.' This is quite true. I also fully agree with La Rochefoucauld: 'It is easier to be wise for others than for yourself.' That, indeed, is the story of my life.

Rereading these early books, I was struck by how little the United States and human nature have changed. The basic passions and attitudes such as competitiveness, conceit, vulgarity, rudeness and kindness are all still there. There are superficial changes, of course. We have moved nearer to America and some of its miracles have reached us: today we too can buy milk in paper containers and light our gas without a match. The biggest difference is that television is not even mentioned in my book – in those days it was radio which dominated the air. But antideluvian though that sounds, the difference is less than it seems at first sight: the cultural advance between the radio soap-opera *My Girl Friday* and the TV soap-opera *Dynasty* is infinitesimal.

To the question 'Shouldn't you bring these books up to date?' I answer 'Of course not.' If they have any value at all it is that they catch a moment in history – the images and attitudes of a particular time. You do not retouch the faces in the family album because the people portrayed have grown older. The little boy on page one may be a grandfather today, but what is interesting is seeing what Grandpapa was like when he was a little boy. And indeed, a careful scrutiny of this present venerable face, and comparison with the childish one in the album, may bring you to the sobering conclusion that he has not changed all that much.

I must admit that I was flattered and delighted when it was suggested that these books should be reprinted. The majority of books live for about six months. Two years is considered a respectable age. So almost forty years can surely count as a bit of immortality? *Hamlet* has survived for four hundred years: *How to Scrape Skies* has survived for forty. Its immortality is one tenth of *Hamlet's*, which is much more than I ever hoped for – and much more than I deserve. But I enjoy being a mini-classic and I shall be grateful to you, Gentle Reader, if your interest adds a year or two to my immortality.

George Mikes

January, 1987

HOW TO SCRAPE SKIES

The United States explored,
rediscovered and explained

'My country, 'tis of thee
Sweet land of liberty,
Of thee I sing;
Land where my fathers died,
Land of the pilgrims' pride,
From every mountain side
Let freedom ring.'

Samuel Francis Smith: America

Portrait of the authors

PREFACE

AFTER the appearance of my little educational treatise *How to be an Alien,* I was bitterly reproached by a number of people for having written the book at all. 'Who wants to be an alien?' people asked me indignantly. 'We all want to be Americans. All of us: the two thousand million non-American population of this earth, children of all ages, continents, sexes and religious denominations; rich and poor, old and young, black and white, small and great. The coming century is going to be the century of the Americans.' 'You are wrong'—I objected—'it is going to be the century of the common man.' 'Same thing,' they retorted. 'Aren't the Americans common enough?'

Well, I have always wanted to be a man with a mission; the only difficulty was deciding what my mission should be. There it was now, my great opportunity—to tell people how to be Americans.

I should like to assure readers before going any further that they may rely on my guidance. I spent two full months in the United States, studying their history, economics, politics, ethnography, constitution, race-problems, legislative, executive and juridical institutions, as well as American social life, geology, genealogy and anthropology. I talked (personally) to many people; travelled across the Manhattan peninsula a dozen times; went for a great number of car and subway rides, visited the Bronx and Queens and reached the outskirts of Brooklyn. What is more, my vision and judgement were not obscured by any previous knowledge of the United States, personal or otherwise.

I travelled widely in New York State; I saw New Jersey, Pennsylvania, Maryland, Washington D.C., Virginia, Connecticut and Massachusetts. I stood at the border and looked right into the depths of West Virginia, and I dare say it looked quite a problem. I talked to people (personally or on the telephone) who had come from as far away as California, Oregon and Washington—without D.C.—and I spent three full days studying the subcontinent of Canada.

Nevertheless, in spite of such thoroughgoing preparation for and devotion to my task, I found myself confronted with certain serious difficulties. First of all, it is not easy to spot America. In New York you will be told that New York is not America. Should you then ask any question concerning the Negro problem in the South, it will be instantly explained to you that the South is not America; New England is so terribly British (because they say tomahto instead of tomayto and sometimes potahto instead of potayto) that it cannot possibly be regarded as America; the Wild West is too wild, the Mid-West is too Mid-Western, and Hollywood—well Hollywood, of course, has never been America. In general, big cities such as Chicago (pronounced Shicago) Philadelphia, Boston, Detroit, Los Angeles, San Francisco etc are not America because America is essentially a rural country; on the other hand, the United States without these vast cities is just not America.

You will find it equally difficult to identify an American. People, all of whose great grand parents were born in the United States, will explain to you that they are Irish, Dutch or Swedes. (Everybody is something else.) The only people who call themselves Americans straightforwardly are those who became citizens five or ten minutes ago.

However, only the superficial observer will be misled into believing that there is no such thing as the United States and the American people. They do indeed exist. They have produced the American constitution, the

American way of life, the comic strips in their newspapers; they have their national game, baseball—which is cricket played with a strong American accent—and they have a national language, entirely their own, unlike any other language spoken on this earth.

On board R.M.S. *Queen Elizabeth*, May 1947

G. M.

Swell guy

I. APÉRITIF

A SWELL GUY

IN America, shoes shine almost as brilliantly as trousers do in post-war England. Only the most careful and determined person can avoid having his shoes cleaned four or five times a day at stands, in shoe-repair shops, at the barber's and in the street. The Americans are a shoe-conscious nation. Only a small band of distinguished, rich and conservative New Englanders try to maintain the noble tradition of dirty shoes, Sunday and weekday rags and an unshaven chin.

In England, I used to be a moderately, or at least tolerably, well-dressed man. Upon my arrival in America, however, my brother besought me urgently to go and buy new clothes; I looked, he said, like a beggar of very mediocre abilities and of the lower beggar income brackets. (In America, everybody belongs to a certain income bracket.)

Here is the rule:

Discard all your shirts and buy new ones—red shirts with huge black checks or, if desired, circles; purple shirts with olive-green butterflies painted all over them, or sky-blue shirts with brown fish. Get some neckties, too—for instance one divided horizontally into blue and golden sections, full of butterflies and fish. Or you may buy a yellow tie with a nude on it, which in electric light becomes still more nude. (For the week-end, of course, you may buy a few odd bits, not quite so conservative as these.)

I must warn all my English readers that American laundries will surprise them. The laundries not only clean your shirts but your linen usually comes back in one piece and not in small instalments. Much pleasurable excitement is lost in that you may rest assured of finding the very same things in your laundry basket that you sent to the laundry. There is no pleasure and expectation in opening a laundry basket, as in England, where you so often find babies' napkins, women's night-gowns and Victorian panties with lots of lace, instead of your dull, unromantic shirts, pants and handkerchiefs.

Have the sleeves of your jacket pressed to a razor edge like the one you have on your trousers. Then, put a tremendous cigar in your mouth. The length of your cigar will be in proportion to your importance. The cigars of those belonging to the lower income brackets hardly exceed two or three feet. In the more modern American cars there is a round hole in the wind-screen so that the driver can stick his cigar through it. In the movie (a movie is in fact an ordinary cinema) you may burn the ears of people sitting in front of you without needing to say 'pardon me'.

Finally you buy a hat. American etiquette is extremely strict concerning hats. You must put on your hat before entering a room, whether in a public or private place. But you must not wear a hat in elevators (ordinary lifts) except in business premises, where you must. Whenever in doubt, leave it on. It is considered rude to take your hat off at any time during your honeymoon, in the bath and at the hairdressers.

WHEN you are dressed, start rushing. Where to does not matter—but rush somewhere, because everybody else is rushing all over the place. There are express lifts and express subway (that is to say underground) trains in America, there are places where you can have a four course lunch in 90 seconds and there are shipbuilding yards which produce two fifty thousand ton battle cruisers or liners every hour; babies, in the upper income bracket circles are produced in three months' time. The production of cheaper babies still takes a little longer.

The American grocer knows but little of the pleasures of an English shopkeeper who may discuss the weather with every single customer for three quarters of an hour on end, while a peaceful and understanding queue stands by, each one awaiting his turn for a friendly chat.

If you believe that London underground trains are crowded in rush hours, you are mistaken. At 9 A.M. or 5 P.M. on the Bakerloo Line between Piccadilly and Oxford Circus you will find a hermit-like solitude compared with a New York subway at the same period of the day. *There* people will placidly sit on your head and settle on your shoulders as pigeons do in the Piazza San Marco in Venice; elderly ladies will crawl about your knees and it is quite customary to find a few odd children in your pockets. When you think the coach is so crowded that it cannot possibly hold one single additional person, at the next station a group of seven cheerful youths will charge it, holding hands and rushing in a body from the requisite distance, till, by the kinetic energy generated, a few superfluous passengers are pushed out on the other side, through the closed doors and windows.

Nobody is angry or irritated. People enjoy themselves and smile kindly. They understand a guy who is in a hurry.

Homeward bound

They work in a hurry, talk in a hurry—in brief, staccato sentences—sleep in a hurry and even drink in a hurry, gulping down impatiently an amazing number of Manhattan cocktails, dry martinis or straight whiskies. They do not enjoy the drink itself, they drink with a purpose: they wish to become reasonably drunk within the shortest period of time possible.

Then you have to get accustomed to the size of things. The Empire State Building has 102 stories and Rocke-feller Centre has more inhabitants—or rather more people working in it—than many large and famous cities in Europe. Texas is three times the area of the United King-dom of Great Britain and Northern Ireland, although the United States itself is only the third largest country on the American Continent. The sugar bowl you find on your table there is a sky scraper in itself. You can see match-boxes which would put a smallish cabin-trunk to shame and each individual match would be quite suitable for use as fire wood in England. If you order southern fried chicken in a restaurant they give you so many pieces that you simply cannot believe it is not southern fried ostrich and you feel disgusted with yourself when you eat it all. The Sunday edition of a newspaper is not unlike a full set of the En-cyclopaedia Britannica, and Coney Island has enough amuse-ment places on top of one another, in a many miles long row, to keep a small Balkan country amused for seven years on end.

A friend of mine, a European painter, not long after his arrival in the United States did a portrait of the president of a huge chain store. The president liked the picture very much and asked how much it cost.

'Two hundred dollars,' my friend replied.

'Good'—the great man nodded. 'And how much would you charge if I ordered several copies?'

My friend was slightly offended but he needed money badly so he asked the president:

'It depends . . . How many copies would you need?'

'Five hundred.'

'I'm sorry . . . I did not quite catch the number.'

'Five hundred, I said. You see, I want my portrait to be hung up in all the offices of my company, all over the United States. But I will not pay you more than a hundred dollars apiece.'

This was more than the artist in my friend could stand:

'But excuse me, sir. . . . I am an artist and not a . . .'

'If you are an artist, do the job quickly,' snapped the great man and the bargain was struck.

That is how a European artist started his career in the United States. Now he specializes in presidents of chain stores and simply refuses to make portraits in less than two hundred copies. He is doing very well. A still life painted by him costs five hundred dollars but if you order a gross you get a twenty per cent reduction.

HOW TO GET GADGET MINDED

THE Americans are extremely gadget minded people and American gadgets have a peculiar characteristic: they work. On the Continent you used to walk up to an automat, drop in a coin, pull a handle and nothing happened. In America you can take a bet that you will get a piece of chocolate or chewing-gum for your cent. I have a streak of altruism in my nature, and personally I prefer the nonchalant Continental automats to the utilitarian American variety—but I admit that this is a matter of taste.

In an American kitchen you find an electric orange squeezer—for making orange juice—and a second mechanical one, just in case the electricity fails. (But electricity never fails.) You also find here an electric dish washer and a clothes washer, a refrigerator and a superb tin opener fixed on the wall; the gas can be lit without using a match or any other lighting device—by simply turning a handle; you will find a high pressure cooker in which you can cook a joint in ten minutes and any vegetable in two or three minutes. I had some cauliflower cooked that way and it really was exactly like the best cabbage I have ever tasted.

There is short shrift for bottles and containers. They have no value and are thrown away. The milk comes in paper bags, lard in jars, cheese in china dishes, flour in small linen bags, tomatoes in cellophane and salt is sold in shakers. These devices make the life of every housewife smooth and easy. They all wish, however, that one single additional device could be invented: domestic help. But that in most cases is quite out of the question.

English people are wise and conservative and strictly opposed to these gadgets which make life prosaic and over mechanised. How right they are, one has to admit, when one thinks of the dull, lifeless and uneventful way the

It works!

Americans heat their houses. Is there anything more exciting, inspiring and—should I say—manly than winter in England? The burst pipe is accepted as a phenomenon of the winter; you know that the pipes *will* burst one day but how exciting it is to spend first of all three pleasant days wrapping them up and then retiring to wait for D-day. How amusing it is to store the coal in a shed, in the garage or in the bath tub, to bring it up in buckets every day to the various rooms, to light fires in the open fireplaces, blow and wait and hold an open newspaper in front of you, swear and pray and do it again when it goes out. Then finally, when it works, the wind comes down the chimney and blows the smoke into the room and you have almost as much trouble in putting the fire out as you had in lighting it. But every day, of course, is not windy. There are cold but peaceful and lovely winter days when, at last, you can lie down on the floor facing your homely, friendly fire and enjoy a really good book; is true that your hair may catch fire if you are careless but you will always have the consolation that your feet get frozen at the same time.

Modern Americans know nothing of these joys of living—they do not even know what they are missing. Their houses have oil heating; which means that a company fills up their tank with oil and all the owner of the house has to do is regulate a meter. This meter is a little clock: it is set to the required temperature—let us say 70°—and when the temperature rises to that point the heating apparatus stops working; if it falls to 69°, it starts up again. In addition to this, the clock can be fixed so that the heating is cut off automatically, let us say at 11 P.M., and restarted at 6 A.M. Poor people—the English reader will think with sympathy —what a dull life they must have! But perhaps . . . No, you are wrong again. The boiler does *not* get dirty and blocked and the whole system does *not* break down twice every year. The oil company, which sells the cheap heating material to you, keeps the boiler clean without any extra charge.

England, as a rule, is a rather warm but very draughty country; America is cold but well-heated. In fact, overheated. On the coldest days, people sit in shirt-sleeves in front of the open windows. Not only the whole of Britain but the whole Continent could be nicely heated with the energy that escapes through the windows in the U.S.

There are automatic waiters in America, automatic parking police which call public attention to you if you park your car for longer than an hour; you can post your letter in a 'mailomat'—which stamps it for you; in restaurants photocell-doors open up automatically before waiters carrying heavy trays; there are automatic cloak-rooms, where you drop in a dime, get a key and close your own section of a steel cupboard. You can drop a dime in a machine which will photograph you, develop and print your picture and deliver it in a frame—all within sixty seconds; you can take out a life insurance policy from an automat and if you put a nickel in a juke-box and press a button, then all the customers in a restaurant have to listen to your favourite tune, maybe twenty times running, whether they like it or not.

I like the system of birthday telegrams, too. For a dollar, I believe, you may send a singing telegram, that is, the telegram boy will deliver it singing 'Happy birthday to you,' calling the addressee, for instance your grandmother, by her Christian name. For ten dollars a choir of ten delivers your telegram and for twenty five dollars the Postmaster General leads the choir.

Various new devices are now under construction:

(1) You push a button and fall in love.

(2) You pull a handle and get married.

(3) You pull a wire and get divorced.

(4) You turn a knob and you may consider yourself to have had a bath.

(5) All classical books to be equipped with a button. You may either read the book or push the button.

There are, however, two serious technical hitches in American life.

(1) A bus-driver is a most unhappy person. He has to do the following things: (a) collect money; (b) give change if required; (c) count the money and transfer it from his collecting box to another from which he can give change more easily; (d) open and close the automatic door; (e) keep a regular check on the number of passengers and his own timetable and (f)—I have almost forgotten this as he himself does occasionally—he has to drive the bus.

(2) In America you need two hands to post a letter. Every letter-box has a handle which you have to pull down; then you throw your letter in and release the handle. You can drive a car, stop a train or fly an aeroplane singlehanded, but you must use both hands to post a letter. If you have a parcel or a suitcase in one hand, you have to put it down to pull the handle.

Now, bus-drivers and letter-posters complain bitterly but American ingenuity has not yet found a way to alleviate their lot. I have two very original—I may even say revolutionary—ideas which may contribute to the solution of these problems. The possibility has occurred to me of employing a second man in the bus, who might perhaps be called the conductor—I think that would be a suitable name for him—who could deal with the passengers so that the driver could give his full attention to driving the bus. Secondly, I reasoned, why not dismantle all those little handles from the pillar-boxes, leaving them with their mouths permanently open so that letters could be thrown in without much strenuous physical effort? After all, the United States is a country of spectacular technical experiments and she may yet give a lead to the world even in this respect.

MANNERS

UNTIL an English or Continental child reaches the mature age of three, his mother cuts up his meat for him, pushes a fork into his right hand and tells him to eat it up. This is the way a well-mannered adult American behaves at table, uniting the parts of mother *and* child. First, he cuts up the meat for himself, then places his knife at the right side of his plate, takes the fork into his right hand and eats.

Table manners are usually quite senseless all the world over. The rules are created by a small class of people who ridicule others for eating differently. Any one class remains the ruling class of a society just as long as it can dictate the rules of handling the knife and fork. In Hungary, people started to bind their table napkins around their necks—in a ridiculous way, so that the table napkins should really protect their clothes—and that meant the end of feudalism in Hungary. In New Guinea a member of a cannibal tribe once cut the ears off a freshly roasted gentleman and—contrary to all tradition—offered them to the chief instead of the priest; next morning the supremacy of priests over the worldly chiefs was broken. In England there will be no serious social revolution as long as the working classes turn their fork upside down and shove their vegetables on top of it.

Table manners make little sense but they always have some reason for coming into existence. If someone took the trouble to psychoanalyse the American nation some interesting conclusions might be reached in the process of finding out why the people of the United States eat like babies of three years of age.

There is an important rule to remember about drinks. Americans have their coffee (always with cream) with the *entrée* and before the sweet (which is not called *sweet* in any case). At every meal you have to drink an immense amount of water, irrespective of whether you drink a dry martini, beer, wine and brandy as well. You swallow some food and immediately drink some water to wash it down. Village schools teach you that you must drink at least three glasses of water per meal; in high schools you are taught to drink at least five; Princeton, Yale and Harvard insist on twelve glasses as the absolute minimum. If you drink less than eight glasses you are considered a man of insufficient education.

But apart from these table rules, American manners are somewhat informal. Everybody is called by his or her Christian name. This is a very democratic habit. You may be called Sir John Soandso, D.S.O., Ph.D., LL.D., head of an important economic mission in the U.S. and anything else if you like, but you simply cannot stand on your dignity if you are introduced to people like this: 'This is John, this is Janet.'

If Mr Albert Einstein is interviewed in front of a microphone, the announcer will introduce him thus: 'Tonight we have in the studio Mr Albert Einstein, the famous scientific guy. Hiya, Albert, it's mighty nice to meet you. I want to ask you a few questions. First of all, Albie, what about relativity? Don't look so worried. Come on, Bertie, don't be shy.'

Friendliness is the general rule. If you are an elevator man and you want to enquire after the health of a tenant's wife, you hail him: 'Hiya Mister—how is the Missus today?' If you look a trifle downcast or worried, the bootblack will pat you on the shoulder and shout into your ear in an encouraging voice: 'Take it easy!'

'Hiya, Al!'

In conversation, you should show a certain human interest in your fellow men   After being introduced to someone, aim at finding out in the first five minutes what his profession is, how much money he makes, what his bank balance amounts to, whether he is faithful to his wife, the name, address, age and profession of his girl friend and whether he has ever cheated the income-tax authorities. When he asks you similar questions, answer frankly, and your open smile should encourage him to make further enquiries into your trade secrets, financial dealings and sex life.

Don't forget that listening to a low pitched voice is a strain on his ear, so shout, roar and howl as loudly as you can; remember on the other hand, that too much talking is a strain on his throat, so interrupt him frequently and save him the trouble of finishing his sentences.

State everything firmly and decisively and discourage contradiction. Do not use expressions like: 'I believe . . .,' ' I shouldn't think so . . .' These phrases are vague and unmanly. If you disagree with anybody's opinion, say bluntly: 'rubbish.' (Or 'garbage' as they call the rubbish in America.)

There is another important American habit you must take note of. The Americans are great letter writers. If you are invited to a party, you must write a letter to the hostess next day saying that you enjoyed her lovely party very much. Whatever happens in a family, you congratulate all the members. You congratulate people at Easter, Christmas and Whitsun. (By the way, the Americans have no bank holidays. Banks—surprising as it may seem—play no part whatever in *their* religious life.) You do not have to possess great literary talent yourself, because you can find printed cards for all possible occasions. In a stationery shop near

Wall Street I collected the following titles at random: Illness, Accidental Illness, Car Accidents, Hospital Illness,
Patriotic Illness, Child Illness, Humorous Illness. (Naturally, I was curious to find out what 'Patriotic Illness' meant
and was thrilled to find a beautiful card with the text: 'Get
well to the tune of *Yankee Doodle Dandy*.' I have unfortunately lost my note about 'Humorous Illness', but as far as I
remember, humorous illness is a kind of indisposition, at the
end of which the patient makes a kick into the air in an extremely humorous way and then dies.) Furthermore: all
sorts of combinations to sister and husband, son and wife,
brother and wife, brother and uncle, daughter and husband,
etc. I saw one section called 'Baby Thank You', with a
special department for twin babies and sub-sections for two
twin boys, two girls, and one boy and one girl. Finally
there were Parting Cards with little pockets for money, to
alleviate the sorrow of the person from whom you part.

While I was looking round, the shopkeeper walked up to
me and asked:

'Can't you find the card you want, Kiddie?'

'No,' I replied. 'I want a greeting card to congratulate
a great grandfather on the occasion of the birth of colour-
blind triplets.'

'Sure'—he nodded seriously, picked out three cards from
his stock, handed them to me and asked:

'Do you want it in English, Italian or Yiddish?'

ENGLISH people will find the American monetary system irritating and confusing. The English have their own simple system: twelve pence make a shilling, twenty shillings a pound, two shillings and sixpence make half a crown but a crown does not exist and two shillings make a florin but this expression is never used. You can explain the English system to any foreigner in five minutes and, if he is a person of extraordinary intelligence, after living two years in this country, he will know how much change he should get from half a crown if he has to pay one and eight.

A dollar, on the other hand, consists of a hundred cents and that's that. I explained to an American business man that the great advantage of the English system is hidden (and how well hidden it is!) in the fact that a pound may be divided into three equal parts—three times six and eight making exactly a pound. That may be very comforting, he replied, but he hardly ever wanted to divide a dollar into three equal parts; on the other hand if he makes a business deal with an English firm, he continued, and makes a profit, let us say, of ten per cent of £35. 17. 10 then he has to employ a specially trained book keeper for half a day to find out the exact amount of his earnings.

There is a complication with the names of the various American coins. A cent is called a penny (but the expressions halfpenny, twopence and threepence do not exist), a five cent piece is a nickel, a ten cent piece a dime, a 25 cent piece a quarter and a 50 cent piece is a half (to rhyme with chaff). A dollar is called a dull'r, the vowel being very long.

The prices of primary necessities are these: a subway ride and a telephone call cost a nickel each; a bus ride costs a

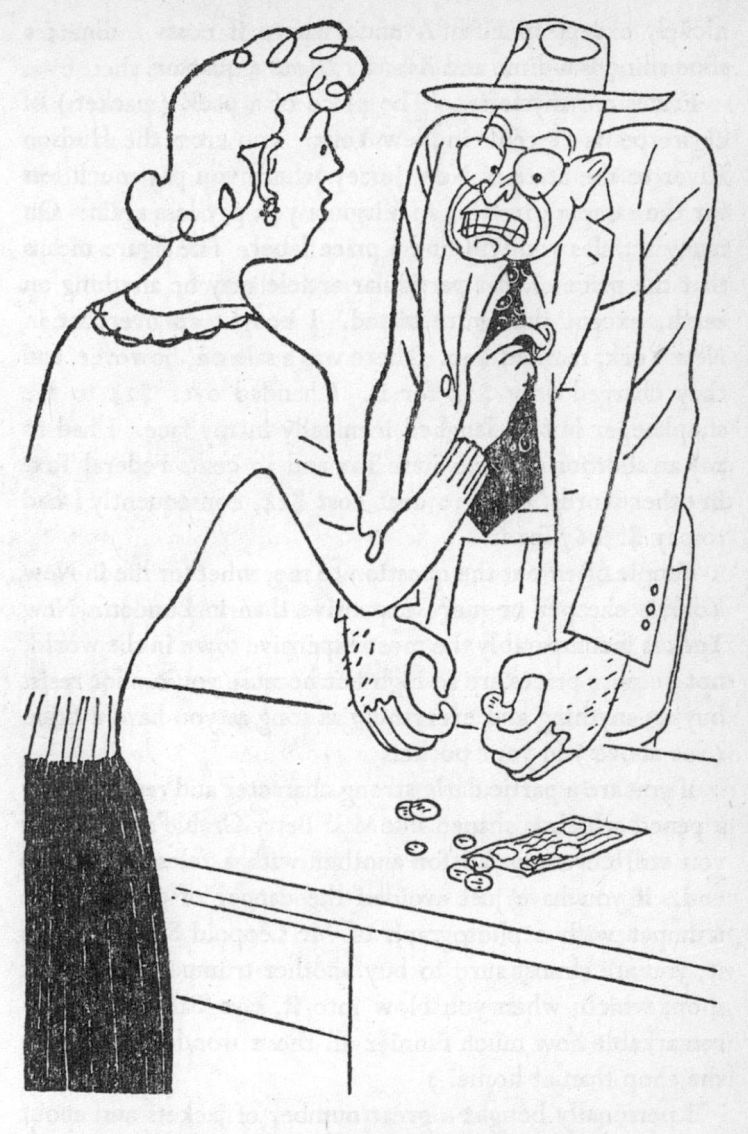

'Sorry, sir, there's no such thing as a one-guinea note!'

nickel, except in Fifth Avenue where it costs a dime; a shoe shine is a dime and *Reader's Digest* a quarter.

Prices are mysteries. The price of a pack (packet) of cigarettes is 18 cents in New York. You cross the Hudson River to the State of New Jersey where you pay much less for the same cigarettes; in Virginia you pay less again. On many articles you will find a price label. The figure means that the price of that particular article may be anything on earth, except the figure stated. I bought an overcoat in New York, marked $30. There was a sale on, however, and they charged only $24 for it. I handed over $24 to the shopkeeper but he laughed ironically in my face. I had to pay an additional $2.30 State Tax and 37 cents Federal Tax. In other words, the $30 coat cost $24, consequently I had to pay $26.67 for it.

People often put the question to me, whether life in New York is cheaper or more expensive than in London. New York is incomparably the most expensive town in the world, not because prices are so high but because you cannot resist buying anything and everything as long as you have a dime (see above) in your pocket.

If you are a particularly strong character and resist buying a pencil which is shaped like Miss Betty Grable's legs, then you will certainly fall for another with a telescope at the end. If you have just avoided the danger of purchasing a trumpet with a photograph of Mr Leopold Stokowski on it, you are almost sure to buy another trumpet in the next shop, which, when you blow into it, says 'Salami'. (It is remarkable how much funnier all these wonders appear in the shop than at home.)

I personally bought a great number of jackets and about half a dozen ball-point fountain pens. Thereupon I firmly

HOW TO SPEND MONEY

decided to stop shopping because I had not too much money left. Next day, I saw a great number of multicoloured fountain pens (80 cents each), all turning around in a shop window, fixed to a red and blue wheel. If it had not been for the wheel, I should have passed the shop with a superior smile on my lips; as it happened, however, I could not resist temptation and bought two more pens. There was a little note attached to one reassuring me that this pen did not leak at a height of 15,000 feet and that I could write with it under water. As I do a considerable amount of writing under water, this was a pleasant surprise to me. I put the new pen in the pocket of my new jacket. The pen leaked. My new jacket was ruined, but as this happened not under water and only ten feet above sea level, the shopkeeper refused to accept responsibility.

SOON after your arrival in the United States, you will see on boards, envelopes and in the newspapers these words often repeated: New York, *N.Y.* . . . 'What does *N.Y.* stand for?' you will enquire. The answer is: New York. 'But you've said it once already, old boy,' you will object. 'We never say London *L.*, or Paris *P.*' You have, however, failed to grasp that the letters *N.Y.* mean that New York City is in New York State and not in Arkansas or Delaware, as the name would suggest. Of course, it is quite possible, even likely, that there are towns of the same name in two or even twenty two states, which is why, when writing down the name of a town or village, you have also to add the abbreviated name of the state, in which it is situated. These abbreviations drive you slightly mad. As long as you do not know the names of forty eight states, you are happy. You see the mysterious sign *Va* or *Ga* and do not care. Then you learn that *Va* stands for Virginia and *Ga* for Georgia and you think you have learnt something. Far from it. Many American states begin with the same letter. There are, for instance, three states beginning with *A*, three beginning with *C*, three with *I*, four with *W*, (not counting Washington D.C., which is not a state), eight beginning with *M* and eight with *N*.

There are certain abbreviations which are not too difficult to learn. I memorised, for example, fairly easily that *Ohio* stands for Ohio, *Iowa* for Iowa and *Utah* for Utah. These are skilful abbreviations which do not put too heavy a strain on a trained memory. You may guess with a certain amount of natural intelligence that *Ariz* indicates Arizona and *Calif* California. But then the *Mi-Mo-Ma* riddle comes in. When you see the sign *Mi*, you have no idea whether it stands for Michigan, Minnesota, Mississipi, or Missouri; you do not know whether the symbol *Ma* stands for Maine, Maryland or Massachusetts. You sigh with relief when you see the abbreviation *Mo*, because it is quite obvious that it can only stand for Montana. The fact that it really stands for Missouri is certainly not your fault.

CONTINENTAL and English people are very fond of old junk. I personally collect all sorts of letters, until they pile up in such a hopeless mess that I have to throw them away—usually together with my most important documents, as it is too much work to sort them out. My mother will never throw away a box. To save room she puts smaller boxes into larger ones and consequently she can never find anything she is looking for—but still, it is so nice to have those useful little boxes in the house. In many homes you will find an old trunk full of family pictures, old clothes, valuable lace and worthless combs, pins, pamphlets and theatre programmes.

Between the American and his material world there is a purely utilitarian relationship. They have the idea that an umbrella, for instance, is there to protect you against rain and not to be cherished as a souvenir. An Englishman will tell you proudly that his car is eleven years old and has done more than 80,000 miles; an American would be ashamed of this. He will, if he can afford it, exchange a perfectly good car for a new one every year. He would not even know the registration number of his automobile as he gets a new licence plate with a new number on it every year.

When it rains, people in America go into a shop and buy a pair of rubber overshoes for a dollar; when it stops raining, they step out of them, leaving the rubber shoes on the pavement. Even the garbage man will not collect them—for his own personal use, I mean. The same happens to umbrellas and if you buy a house, you are sure to find a lot of very good furniture and carpets in it (not included in the price, of course) because the former owner just would not take the trouble of removing them. Very often you see advertisements in the paper, announcing that if you are prepared to collect a piano at such and such an address, you may keep it.

The Americans discard whole cities in the same way. When a town has served its purpose—the gold rush is over, or a mine in the neighbourhood has been exhausted—they evacuate it, leaving houses and furniture behind. You can find a great number of ghost towns all over the place. There is no silly sentimentalism: 'Right or wrong, my own city'. If it is right—it is my own city; if it is wrong, I move to a better place.

The United States is certainly not a second hand country. They are not sentimental over old pants and old books. Occasionally they buy some antique stuff, provided it is in rather good condition and fairly new. Traditions? Their tradition is to have always the best, the most modern and most practical of everything. Grandfather clocks may chime midnight beautifully, usually at 25 minutes past 2 A.M.; *their* electric clocks are ugly, unromantic, have no history and no patina and they would be utterly useless but for the fact that they always show the right time.

HOW TO HAVE FUN

To be able to enjoy life in the United States, you must become kind-hearted and easy-going. The Americans are truly kind and good-tempered people, always ready to help others. Once, when I was using the 'mailomat'—the machine which stamps and posts your letters—at one of the railroad stations,* I dropped my dime into the slot reserved for pennies only. The machine did not work and a man walked up to me to ask what the matter was. I told him and urged him not to worry; I would drop another dime into the right slot and that would solve my problem. 'No, Sir,' he declared firmly and in two minutes about a dozen people —civilians and railwaymen and postmen—surrounded the machine, punching, pushing, beating, boxing, caressing, coaxing and kicking it, until it was cowed into submission and returned my dime. Then they showed me the right way to use the mailomat and my letter disappeared at the proper place, accompanied by the cheers and good wishes of the crowd. I thanked them for their help and remarked: 'It must be very interesting to see one's own letter stamped by this machine.' I merely wanted to make some conversation and nothing more brilliant occurred to me. 'Wait a minute, Sonnie,' said one of the postmen, which surprised me as I was wearing a beard in those days. The postman disappeared and returned a few seconds later with a key, opened the machine, looked for my letter and handed it to me very proudly. People are in a hurry, that is true; but they are always prepared to stop, help and please others. In England if you ask someone about a street, he will politely tell you where it is; or more likely, he will reply in a very civil tone that he is afraid he does not know. In America the person accosted may ask you why you want to get there. You will

* It was an ordinary railway station in fact

'*I'm a stranger here meself*'

tell him that you heard about an apartment (flat) which may be available there. Then he will accompany you to the address mentioned, will bargain with the landlord, hire the apartment for you, help to move in your heavier furniture and disappear before you have a chance of thanking him properly.

The primary purpose in life, for many millions of Americans is to 'have fun' or 'to have a kick out of life'. 'Having fun' is no complicated process. The movie is the greatest fun of all; dancing, playing cards, skating, or necking (kissing in a car with anybody, anywhere and at any time) is fun; looking at pictures in a magazine and drinking orange juice is also great fun. They are satisfied with everything and enjoy everything. To meet Mr Peter Lorre in the street is a real treat; to listen to an awful crooner in a second rate restaurant is a kick ; to witness a nice car accident is just too wonderful for words.

Years ago in London I knew a little English girl, called Eileen. She told me once: 'Me and my girl friend have such a wonderful sense of humour. We sit down and laugh for hours on end. without the slightest reason.'

I often thought of little Eileen in the United States of America.

NOT IDENTICAL . . .

IN Continental newspapers one can often see so-called 'not identical' notices. If a law-abiding citizen happens to have the same name as a criminal, he inserts a 'not identical' notice in the paper in order to avoid any misunderstanding. For example:

I, the undersigned John Horn, am not identical with Mr John Horn who was hanged this morning in the courtyard of Marko prison.

John Horn, hatmaker
23 Church Street

Often these notices refer not to criminals, but on the contrary, to honest, or sometimes even distinguished members of society. People are jealous of their identity and do not wish to be taken for anybody else. We all know that both Winston Churchill the writer and Winston Churchill the statesman were anxious to let the world know who is who and worked out an arrangement for signing their names differently.

I often thought of these 'not identical' notices while in America. I was personally held responsible for Britain's foreign policy, warned about the dangers of imperialism, told off for being anti-Russian and then reprimanded for being too much pro-Russian. I got into most serious trouble because of the British government's Palestine policy. People tried to persuade and convince me, threaten, cajole and beg of me; somebody declared most emphatically that the Jews and Arabs would understand one another like brothers but for the British who sow discord between them. An elderly gentleman drew me aside at a party, dragged me into another room, closed the door and besought me:

'Give it to the Jews.' I was so touched by his deep emotion and obvious sincerity that I was on the verge of giving it to the Jews, when I realised, at the very last moment, that I had to be firm.

I should like to take this opportunity of communicating the following announcement to all concerned:

I, the undersigned, am not identical with the Right Hon. Ernest Bevin, His Majesty's Secretary of State for Foreign Affairs.

George Mikes

II. MANHATTAN

THE CITY

MANHATTAN is, first of all, the name of a very popular cocktail. Secondly, it is the name of an island which forms the heart of New York N.Y. The island is thirteen miles long, two miles wide and lies at the mouth of the Hudson River. East of it runs the East River, which divides the island from Long Island. Manhattan covers 54·4 square miles and has a population of 1,889,924. It is also one of the five boroughs (or, as the Americans prefer to spell it, *boros*) of New York City and for the foreigner it *is* New York City. I do not intend to insult the population of the Bronx, Queens, Richmond and Brooklyn, but for the visitor New York N.Y. means skyscrapers, the Empire State Building, Rockefeller Center, tremendous traffic, dazzling neon advertisements, Central Park, Times Square, Harlem, the avenues and famous streets—and all these are to be found in Manhattan.

New York was first seen by an Italian navigator, Giovanni de Verrazano, in 1524. The city, originally called New Amsterdam, was a Dutch possession and it was the New Netherlands Company which was granted a charter for exclusive trading rights. The Dutch had considerable trouble with the administration of the new community, so the English with their customary readiness to help people in trouble, rid them of all their worries by taking the colony over by force in the seventeenth century. New Amsterdam was renamed New York. Manhattan island itself was purchased by the Dutch from Indians in 1626. It seems that estate prices were pretty low at that time.

New York is built in such a way that a great deal of amusement and fun, to which inhabitants of English towns are accustomed, is lost. Parallel streets were discovered in England in 1923 but most of the towns had already been built. An English town is not simply the communal dwelling place of a number of citizens, it is also an elaborate quiz; you cannot simply 'pass through' an English town, you have to solve it. Try to make a 'short cut' in an imperfectly known district, relying on your infallible sense of direction, and the Lord have mercy upon your soul! If you land in a *cul-de-sac* you are lucky; you are much more likely to find yourself in a cork screw street in which you twist and turn like a snake dancer until, fifteen minutes later, you are faced with the diverting task of extricating yourself from the utterly strange regions into which you have penetrated. Travellers like to thrill us with their tales about the difficulties and horrors of Himalayan exploration. I am not impressed. The Himalayas cannot possibly offer any problems until the English build a few carefully planned towns on them.

All this excitement and *joie de vivre* is lost in New York. Manhattan is full of parallel rows of buildings, those running from north to south being called avenues while those running from east to west are called streets.

The avenues and streets have only numbers instead of names. On the Continent streets are usually named after historic figures and politicians. Every twenty five years there is a revolution and a change of régime and then all the streets are re-christened and very often it is a criminal offence to call them by their former names. Sometimes even the postmen have no idea what the various streets in their district are called and occasionally people are not quite sure

Plus ça change, plus c'est la même chose

about the current names of the very streets they live in.
These pleasures can never mean anything to the American.
Régimes may come and go, the Republicans may take over
from the Democrats and vice versa, new parties may gain
or lose power, but 21st Street will keep its name under the
most conservative or most revolutionary régime alike.

This is not the only disadvantage of the system. In London
it may fall to your lot to find Alma Square N.W.8. You
have a vague idea where it may be and ask seventy eight
different persons and nobody knows exactly where Alma
Square is. Bus-men who have driven past in its immediate
neighbourhood for twenty eight years, have never heard of
it. People who pass through it twice a day, only know that
it is somewhere near, either in front of you or behind you,
either to the left or—maybe—to the right. How nice it is
to discover after two hours' research, just when you are
about to give the whole thing up, that you have passed
through Alma Square ten times during your tour, only

> (a) there are no new name placards, and (b) the
> old placards which say 'Wellesley Gardens' went out of
> date seven years ago and should have been utterly dis-
> regarded.

You feel a sense of triumph and superiority after finding
Alma Square; but who on earth will feel a sense of triumph
in New York on finding 79th Street between 78th and 80th
Streets? Let the British build a town with numbered streets
and *then* try to find 79th Street in it!

The English influence has, however, scored minor vic-
tories in New York. Broadway, for example, betrays every
aspect of the independent British spirit. It has no number
but a name; it is not at all straight, but it bends and curves

and twists like a whimsical rattlesnake, all along the length of Manhattan. You walk uptown in Sixth Avenue and at 30th Street Broadway is to your right; you reach 40th Street and Broadway is to your left; at Central Park South it decides to take a sharp turn to the west and it passes the line of Eleventh Avenue, then still further up it turns back eastward again. You can play an exhilarating game of hide and seek with Broadway and always Broadway wins.

The English town planning spirit gained a few points around the Avenues, too. If you have numbers instead of names, the idea would be that Second Avenue should follow First, Third Avenue Second and so on. This belief is too naïve. Between Third and Fourth they succeeded in smuggling in a quite superfluous little avenue called Lexington. Half of Fourth Avenue is called Fourth Avenue, the upper part of it is called Park Avenue. Between Fourth and Fifth Avenues there is a further annoying phenomenon, named Madison Avenue, and then, between Fourth and Eleventh Avenues, Broadway. The Sixth Avenue as such has recently been abolished and renamed 'Avenue of the Americas'. Nobody ever speaks of the 'Avenue of the Americas', on the other hand no official sign acknowledges the fact that there is or ever was a Sixth Avenue. You will be directed by someone to walk along Sixth Avenue and you do not find Sixth Avenue; you find the Avenue of the Americas instead which, in turn, may not be shown on your map.

These oases of muddle are certainly appreciated by visitors from England. But all attempts at improvement are futile; New Yorkers have committed a basic error in planning Manhattan in such a logical way and all subsequent efforts, however noble, are wasted; Manhattan just missed its chance of becoming a second Soho.

THE Americans are a dynamic people. Consequently they prefer a dynamic muddle to a static muddle. In New York you may know indeed where you *are* but they have built a huge intricate subway system with the sole aim in view that you should not know how to get from where you are to any other place. The buses do auxiliary duties and as a neo-American friend declared to me: he had often been miscarried.

To travel by car would be comparatively easy, but nobody uses his car in New York, because so many people use it that traffic is congested and unbearably slow. So you try the bus.

I was accustomed to take a Number 4 at Pennsylvania Station and ride to Fifth Avenue. One day I discovered a Number 4 bus in Lexington Avenue and got in, but instead of arriving at Fifth Avenue I found myself somewhere in the Middle West. The driver laughed at me when I explained my case to him, because—he told me—I had taken a Lexington Avenue 4 instead of a Fifth Avenue 4. I learned later that they have many Number 4 buses in the town, so by skilful economy they save the use of several figures every year. These figures are given to charity at the end of the year, in one lump sum.

Next day I tried the subway. At Pennsylvania Station I boarded a subway train marked: 49th Street. That was exactly what I wanted. I started reading my newspaper and did not notice that at the next stop, at 42nd Street, all the passengers got out, leaving me alone in the whole train. The train started moving again but stopped in the tunnel and went on shunting up and down for about forty minutes. The conductor walked through the carriage three or four times, saw me there in my melancholy solitude but said nothing.

On his next appearance I asked him:

'When do we reach 49th Street?'

He laughed jovially:

'49th Street? But we ain't going to 49th Street. Why should we?'

'Excuse me, sir, I never suggested that you should if you don't feel like it. I only saw a board on this train saying that it *was* going to 49th Street and that gave me the foolish idea that it might be going to 49th Street. My fault, I admit.'

He became indignant.

'Everybody knows you got to change at 42nd.'

'I didn't know.'

'You didn't?' he said in an ironical tone. 'How long have you been living in New York?'

'Two days.'

'Two days', he shouted triumphantly. 'Then you couldn't possibly have known.'

On another occasion, I asked the subway official at an 8th Avenue subway station how to get to Columbus Circle. 'Take the train here'—he smiled—'and get off at Columbus Circle.' I took the train there, reached 34th Street, then 42nd, then 50th and, as Columbus Circle is at 59th, I thought everything was mighty swell. Then some irregularities occurred. We reached a station called Seventh Avenue, then Fifth Avenue, then Lexington Avenue. Then we started moving again, did not stop for fifteen minutes and finally reached 23rd Street, Long Island City, which is on the eastern hemisphere. There I got out and told my story to an official. He found it entertaining and explained to me that I ought to have taken an *A* train instead of an *E* train, or an *E* train instead of an *A* train, or an *AA* train instead of an *FZ* train.

'But how could I have guessed that?' I asked him in despair.

'Everybody knows that,' he retorted with a superior smile on his lips and turned away from me with contempt in his heart.

All these closely guarded secrets would have been given away long ago had they not taken further security measures.

(1) In most cases they do not mark the various lines on which the stations lie. If they mark the line, they mark it in such a way that the boards should mislead the more naïve type of passenger. Seventh Avenue Subway is called Seventh Avenue Subway at one point but at the next station it is called I.R.T.-line. 'Everybody knows' that I.R.T. stands for Interboro' Rapid Transportation System (T meaning both Transportation and System), and this is just a colloquial name for the Seventh Avenue line. At 34th Street you will see B.M.T.-line and 8th and 6th Avenue trains are often called 'Ind Subway', meaning Independent Subway which is just a cute way of telling the public that the line is not independent, because all subway lines belong to the city.

(2) Subway maps are as closely guarded as military secrets. You cannot find a subway map at any station. You can find maps *inside* the carriages and there you can find out which subway you should have boarded instead of the one you actually did board. Those maps, too, show only that particular line on which you are travelling and if you want to change, you are absolutely free to choose a new line, wherever and whenever you wish.

In the New York subway system there are parallel tracks for local trains and express trains. The local train stops at every station, the express only at every fifth or sixth station. I always travelled by express. If I do not know in any case —I reasoned—where I shall arrive, at least I wish to arrive there as quickly as possible.

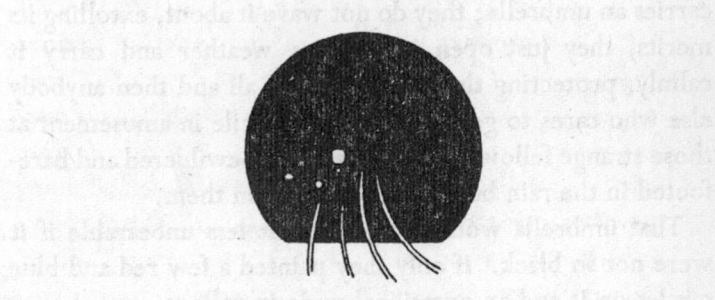

MANY Americans dislike the English because—they say—the English have an uppish and superior attitude towards the rest of humanity. The English have not created a civilisation in the sense that ancient Greece and Renaissance Italy did, but, as it happens, they have been the flag-bearers of modern Western civilisation for the last few decades. They carry that flag as a well-disciplined country gentleman carries an umbrella; they do not wave it about, extolling its merits, they just open it in rainy weather and carry it calmly, protecting themselves first of all and then anybody else who cares to get under it; they smile in amusement at those strange fellows who rush around bewildered and barefooted in the rain but pass no remark on them.

That umbrella would be somewhat less unbearable if it were not so black. If only they painted a few red and blue circles on it and an occasional nude in yellow.

In America this superior attitude is quite unknown. Nobody looks down upon anybody; all men and women are considered equal with the following exceptions:

There are a great number of people of Anglo-Saxon descent who look down upon the rest of the community. The ancestors of these people came over in the *Mayflower*. One of these *Mayflower* people once boasted to a refugee about his ancient roots in America, upon which the refugee retorted: 'But *I* came here when there was already a strict immigration control in force.' Another person once remarked: 'My ancestors came over in the *Mayflower*.' To which another replied: 'And my ancestors were on the reception committee.' (He was an Indian.)

The *Mayflower*, by the way, was a vast ship of 85,000 tons and made innumerable trips between Southampton and

'Pleased to meet you!'

Plymouth (New England): that is how so many people crossed in her.

Furthermore all white people look down upon Mulattoes;

all Mulattoes look down upon Negroes;

all Negroes look down upon Mulattoes;

all people of Scandinavian origin look down upon Germans;

all Germans look down upon Central Europeans;

all Central Europeans look down upon Italians, Spaniards, Armenians and Persians;

all Italians and Spaniards look down upon Central Europeans and Irish;

all of them look down upon Jews;

all Jews look down upon everybody else;

all Americans look down upon New Yorkers;

all New Yorkers look down upon Mid-Westerners and Wild-Westerners;

all Northern people look down upon Southerners;

all Southerners look down upon the 'Yanks'.

All emigrants look down upon the refugees (an emigrant is a refugee who arrived before 1933, a refugee is an emigrant who arrived after that date). All refugees look down upon those who arrived in a later ship and if people came in the same ship those who got off first look down upon the newcomers whose luggage was examined a little later.

All those who are 'citizens' look down upon those who have only just got their 'first papers'. Those with their first papers look down upon the pseudo-visitors who are trying to settle in the United States.

It is easy to see that the people looked down upon most by others in the United States are Yiddish speaking Negro Jewish refugees with expired visitors' visas.

HOW TO BE A PRESSURE GROUP

NEW York is the second largest city in the world. New York is a provincial town; it is not the capital of the United States and not even the capital of New York State.

In our eyes New York is a solid American city. Writers have tried to define a 'nation' on racial, historical and economic grounds—and failed mostly because the United States and Switzerland defy all definition. I believe it is fair to say that a nation consists of people who read the same newspapers, listen to the same radio programme, play the same games and hold their knife and fork in the same way. In that sense New York is a hundred per cent American. At the same time more Britishers live in New York than in Brighton or Birkenhead, almost as many Irish as in Dublin, more Germans than in Cologne, more Poles than in Cracow, more Austrians than in Salzburg, as many Hungarians as in Szeged, more Russians than in Kiev, more Italians than in Naples, more Negroes than in South West Africa and more than five times as many Jews as in Palestine.

An American and a New York way of life is superimposed on the whole community but underneath it, or parallel with it, the various communities live their own lives and everybody seems to be proud of his origin. The day following my arrival in New York, I went for a walk in Chinatown, entered a shop, and there was a dairyman, sitting chatting with the Chinese proprietrix. He started talking to me in that outspoken and straightforward American fashion:

'Are you Jewish? Because you look Jewish.'

Then he looked at me again and declared:

'No, you don't look Jewish, but you look like a refugee.'

'Thank you,' I nodded with appreciation.

'You are dressed like a refugee.'

'No doubt.' (I had my best English suit on.)

'No offence meant.'

'No offence taken.'

'I am Jewish myself.'

'Are you?'—I exclaimed with surprise.

'Sure.   And I am proud of it.'

I turned to the Chinese woman but before I had an opportunity of telling her what I wanted, the dairyman continued the conversation.

'What are you?'

'I am proud, too.'

'I mean it. What are you?'

'I am a Polish Negro.'

'But you are white.'

'Yeah. Not so white as you think.'

'White enough.'

'Didn't you know? In Europe Negroes *are* white.'

He would not take it.

'You're kidding. When did you arrive here?'

'Yesterday.'

'Only yesterday? But you speak very good English.'

'I've been living in London.'

'In London? Do they speak English there, too?'

'Kinda English,' I declared firmly and the conversation was closed.

All these national communities are settled in separate districts. In Yorkville you see German boards on the shops with German names on them, German newspapers are sold in the streets, German films are shown in the cinema and you may walk up to anybody, address him in German and the chances are nine to one that he would reply in German.

Big chain stores in this district would not employ an assistant if he did not speak German fluently. The same description applies to any other national district and if you turn the dial on your radio slowly around, you are certain to hear commercials sung in Yiddish and Spanish, in Swedish and Armenian and scores of other European and Asiatic languages. There are craftsmen of so many nationalities in New York that you can get anything on earth in the shops and restaurants. Rumanian peasant dresses, Venetian glass, Marseilles bouillabaisse, Italian salami, Pilsen beer, Chinese back scratchers—and all a shade better than the original.

In most cases the children of these people learn the American language perfectly but sometimes they speak only their ancestors' mother tongue even unto the second or third generation. You find people seventy five years old, who were born in New York, never left the city boundaries and who speak only Ukrainian or Schwitzerdeutsch. Occasionally rather unexpected things occur. Three years ago my brother, then still in uniform, was driving through Brunswick, New Jersey—a town with a large Hungarian population. Having lost his way, he stopped in front of a house and asked a little Negro boy, in English, how he could reach the main road. The boy turned away, opened the gate and shouted to his mother in Hungarian, with a broad Transdanubian accent: 'Mother, come quick, there is a soldier here.'

All these people are or will become citizens. It is true, they always retain a certain interest in their country of origin, but their loyalty to the United States is unquestionable.

Luckily there is no patriotism of the sort one saw, for instance, in pre-war Italy. I never heard or read a word about 'our beloved, sacred country'. Every now and then they speak of the American flag and they all adore the 'American way of life'—which in their eyes seems to be a matter of honour; in ours it is a matter of taste. They are all grateful to the country which gave them freedom and grapefruit, a high standard of living and the comic strips in the newspapers, employment and chewing-gum, Abraham Lincoln and Frank Sinatra. They are all citizens, except the 333,000 Indians, who I believe are considered visitors.

Abraham, son of Kentucky

HOW TO SHOP

IN America, just as in England, you see the same shops with the same boards and windows in every town and village.

Shopping, however, is an art of its own and you have to learn slowly where to buy various things. If you are hungry, you go to the chemist's. A chemist's shop is called a drug-store in the United States; it is a national institution and a very good institution at that. In the larger drug-stores you may be able to get drugs, too, but their main business consists in selling stationery, candy, toys, braces, belts, fountain pens, furniture and imitation jewellery. Every drug-store has a food counter with high stools in front of it and there they serve various juices, coffee, sundaes, ice cream, sandwiches, omelettes and other egg dishes. A friend of mine in Hollywood met Otto Hapsburg, the claimant to the Austrian-Hungarian throne, who—I understand—apart from his hobby of calling himself a king, is an extremely charming and cultured young man. My friend called on Otto one morning in his hotel. He was received by the *aide-de-camp* who declared ceremoniously:

'*Seine Majestät nimmt sein Frühstück in der Apotheke.*' (His Majesty is having his breakfast in the pharmacy.)

If you want cigarettes, go to the grocer; if you want to have your shoes cleaned, go to the barber; if you want a radio, go to a man's shop; if you want a suitcase, go to the chemist's. On the other hand if you want to send a telegram, avoid the post office, because telegrams are handled by private companies. Nor has the post office anything to do with the telephone either, as telephone service is supplied by the American Telephone and Telegraph Co. Nor will you find public conveniences in America in the British sense of the word because a lavatory is a strictly private enterprise in the United States.

Whatever you buy, it may be exchanged later for something in the same shop. This is a great pastime with the Americans. A great many people do not really buy things —they only acquire some raw material for later exchanges. It is not unusual at all to see a lady bringing back a hat with a lot of fruit on it and exchanging it either for real fruit or a real hat; or to see somebody bringing back a refrigerator with the remark that he made a mistake and now he wants to subscribe to the *Reader's Digest* instead.

You do not need to time your shopping very carefully because you will find some shops stay open in New York all night. The big department stores keep open till 9 P.M. once a week. Should you want a meal at any time of the day or night, that is quite easy. If you have a party in your house and you decide at 2.30 A.M. to have some music, you can rush down to the corner, buy a piano and it will be delivered to your home within half an hour. If you fancy playing golf at 3.45 in the morning you can purchase, if you wish, a set of golf clubs and balls. I still cannot quite decide what to do with that Indian feather head-dress I bought one morning at 5.15 in Greenwich Village, but I was deeply impressed by the tempting opportunity and could not resist buying it.

You must be extremely careful concerning the names of certain articles. If you ask for suspenders in a man's shop, you receive a pair of braces, if you ask for a pair of pants, you receive a pair of trousers and should you ask for a pair of braces, you receive a queer look.

I should like to mention that although a lift is called an elevator in the United States, when hitch-hiking, you do not ask for an elevator, you ask for a lift.

There is some confusion about the word *flat*. A flat in America is called an apartment; what *they* call a flat is a puncture in your tyre (or as they spell it, *tire*). Consequently the notice: FLATS FIXED does not indicate an estate agent where they are going to fix you up with a flat, but a garage where they are equipped to mend a puncture. Only once did I see this popular notice, FLATS FIXED, on a shop which sold brassières. The customary slogan for these establishments is: 'United we stand, divided we fall'.

An average English motorcar could be placed, I believe, without much difficulty, in the luggage-rack of an average American automobile. A well-known, but rather small English 8 h.p. car is on show in a window in 42nd Street and is exceedingly popular with the entire population. There is always a huge crowd in front of the shop window and everybody is roaring with laughter. 42nd Street is the movie street in New York and if people cannot get into the cinema, they spend an hour or two in front of that shop window and consider their excursion well worth while.

'Seeing the car' is a regular item of all sight-seeing tours, too. I was deeply hurt when a veteran who had served in England explained to his friends:

'These little things, you know, have to run on the *roads* in England. I think it's very unfair. They should not be allowed to get off the pavement.'

I talked to an English motorcar expert over there, who had something to do with that show too, and asked him, who on earth bought these cars in the United States, considering that they are not cheaper than a 30 h.p. Chevrolet.

'They are moderately popular in the country.'

'In the country of Great Britain and Northern Ireland you mean?' I enquired.

'No, I mean here in the various States. In Oregon, for instance, they are very much appreciated.'

'I see . . . That is why you exhibit them in New York. A jolly good idea, particularly if you come to think of the fact that New York is practically as far from Oregon as it is from London.'

'That is a good point,' he nodded. 'A very good point indeed. Distances *are* amazing in this country, aren't they?'

In the United States the price of steel is much lower than in Britain, mass production methods are much cheaper, petrol is very much cheaper (which is important because the consumption of these huge cars is very high) and there is no horse-power tax. One has to pay a certain amount according to the weight of the car for one's licence plate every year—that is all.

An American car is as big as a railway engine. There is a radio set in every car, cigar lighter, electric heater, air conditioner, a set of openly placed and hidden lights, nylon seat covers, electrically operated windows and convertible seats which may be used as beds. Now they are experimenting with a view to introducing running hot and cold water, baths and a foot-bath for the driver for hot days, an elevator and a crane to save passengers from the fatigue of using their own feet when getting in and out. In spite of all these devices and gadgets, they still find a cute way of placing the engine somewhere. These motors are terrific—in New York and other big towns they are able to crawl at a speed of eight miles per hour without much trouble and in fact no speed is too slow for them. It is much more difficult on the highways where real skill, energy and determination is needed to keep a low speed. There are only fifteen states where you may drive faster than 50 m.p.h., at no single point in any state is the speed limit removed and in Washington D.C. you must not exceed 25 m.p.h. Still it is fun thinking how fast you *could* go in these modern marvels, if only you could go fast.

Modern American cars have no starter, or to put it more clearly, the starter is built together with the gas-pedals. You turn the ignition key, push the gas-pedal down and the motor starts. And it *does* start, mind you. An American friend asked me whether I still had a starter on my English car.

'Oh no. . . . No starter on my car . . .' I replied and changed the subject.

This was the truth but not the whole truth. The whole truth is that my starter broke about a year ago and was removed and now I always have to use the handle when I want to start the car. No starter—no starter. You may use different means for achieving the same end.

The forty eight states of America have varying laws relating to motor vehicles, which fact does not make the motorist's life any happier. In Alabama you have to apply for a new licence plate on October 1. In Ohio on March 1, in New York on January 1 and in California on January 2. In Louisiana you may start driving at the age of fourteen, in Vermont you must be at least eighteen. Driving tests differ everywhere and in three States no driving licence is required at all. In some states you may stay for ninety days with your home licence plate, in others only for twenty five. But these are only minor difficulties. The real trouble arises when, driving through a 'foreign' state you make a U-turn, for instance. (A U-turn is a full turn in a street.) In some streets you are only supposed to make a Y-turn. (A Y-turn is a turn where you shuttle backwards and forwards and this expression does not exist at all—but I feel it should exist.) Then you may be put in jail on a Saturday afternoon and kept there until Monday morning on the excuse that the sheriff is away for the week-end, or too busy to deal with your case. On Monday morning, as a rule, you have the choice of paying one, twenty, fifty or a hundred dollars fine

The girl who took the wrong turning

or of waiting for the decision of a higher court, the only difficulty being that you have to wait for it in jail. A friend of mine just rushed down in Atlanta, Georgia, to buy a couple of aspirins for his wife at 3.14 P.M. on a Saturday and returned at 11.17 A.M. on Monday without the aspirins, having spent all his money on an expensive but not very entertaining U-turn.

To fine 'foreign' motorists is not only an exciting pastime but a safe and permanent income for certain towns and many people are quite prepared to make a forty or fifty mile detour to avoid a certain city because they know that the sheriff there is fond of unusually long week-ends. I met one gentleman who bought an aeroplane and flies to his office every morning from a nearby town because the air, for the time being at any rate, is free of troopers—i.e. state traffic police.

The American roads are the best in the world. Wide, safe highways cut across the big cities and the whole country and there are no traffic lights and no cross-roads anywhere. Cross-roads run either above or underneath the highways and side-tracks always lead up or down to them.

Parking is perhaps even more difficult in New York than it is in London. The police used to be bullied in both cities because parking cars blocked so many roads. One ingenious New York police official found a solution to this problem and forbade parking in a number of streets. This example was readily and swiftly followed in London. Now people know they must not park in certain streets. But where should they park? The police shrug their shoulders. There is plenty of space on the moon. In New York, even garages are full, but it is strictly forbidden to keep a car in the street overnight. Garages, however, when they cannot find room for all the cars on their premises, *are* allowed to keep cars in the street. So this situation has arisen: you pay the garage a high fee to have your car under shelter during the night, in return for which fee, you may keep it in the street.

IT was decided almost two hundred years ago that English should be the language spoken in the United States. It is not known, however, why this decision has not been carried out.

HOW TO GO BANKRUPT

IF you feel like going bankrupt, do not hesitate to do so. There is no stigma, or even blame attached to it. It is true that success is the measure of what you are worth; but you cannot achieve success without trying hard and it is obvious to every American that a number of experiments are bound to fail. The foundation of American commercial life is credit. It is easy to obtain credit. It is easy to open—let us say—a modern barber's shop with seventy five chairs, equipped with hair drying, hair washing and massage machines, X-ray and ultra-violet apparatus and with a huge surgery where one or two barbers (who are not very good at shaving) remove tonsils and appendices much cheaper than the neighbouring hospital. Yes, it is easy to open such an establishment on credit but you must pay the instalments or you are lost.

But you are not 'lost' in the English or Continental sense. On the Continent, ruin means ruin; the possibilities are extremely limited. All the people in a certain branch of business know one another or at least know of one another and there is little chance of recuperating, or at any rate, it needs exceptional energy, perseverance and doggedness. In England again, it is the moral side of the question that is so difficult to bear. A person who is unable to meet his liabilities, in most cases feels a fallen man. In plutocratic America, money means money—openly and brazenly; in England, money, for a newly grown up and incurably snobbish middle-class, means social status and when bankruptcy brings home the harsh fact that this social status was based primarily or exclusively on money—that, usually, has a crushing moral effect. For the American, a temporary and transitory status of bankruptcy does not mean more than a 'nasty morning' means for the English. It is nasty today, it will probably be nasty tomorrow and the day after tomorrow but a week today—well, we shall see. . . . Commercial life on the whole is just as scrupulously honest in the United States as it is in Britain. But every moneylending firm is prepared for a certain percentage of loss. If the proprietor of the barber shop cannot pay the instalments, the shining, silvery machines will be dismantled, the X-ray and ultra-violet apparatus wrapped up carefully and carried away and the surgery delivered to the neighbouring hospital. The ex-barber smiles and takes it easy. For a few months per-haps he will sell ice cream in the street, clean shoes or take a job as a radio commentator on international affairs and then he tries again—this time manufacturing honey (sold in tubes), or fertilisers or producing a psycho-analytical magazine. I do not intend to convey the idea that every rich American becomes bankrupt twice every year; but this sort of thing certainly occurs periodically to a great number of people.

A person may have been working in an office for 37 years and then one Saturday he may be informed by the boss that his services are not required any more and he should not take the trouble to come in on Monday next. The question of notice, let alone pension, does not arise. Or a person who may have flourished as a toothpaste manufacturer for two decades, may find himself one day busily trying to found a little firm in order to export children's underwear to Chile.

America is called a country of unlimited possibilities. We have heard so many stories of the little boot-black who finished his life as a good, wise, multi-millionaire steel manufacturer, newspaper magnate or refrigerator king. It is rarely mentioned that there is a two-way traffic on these

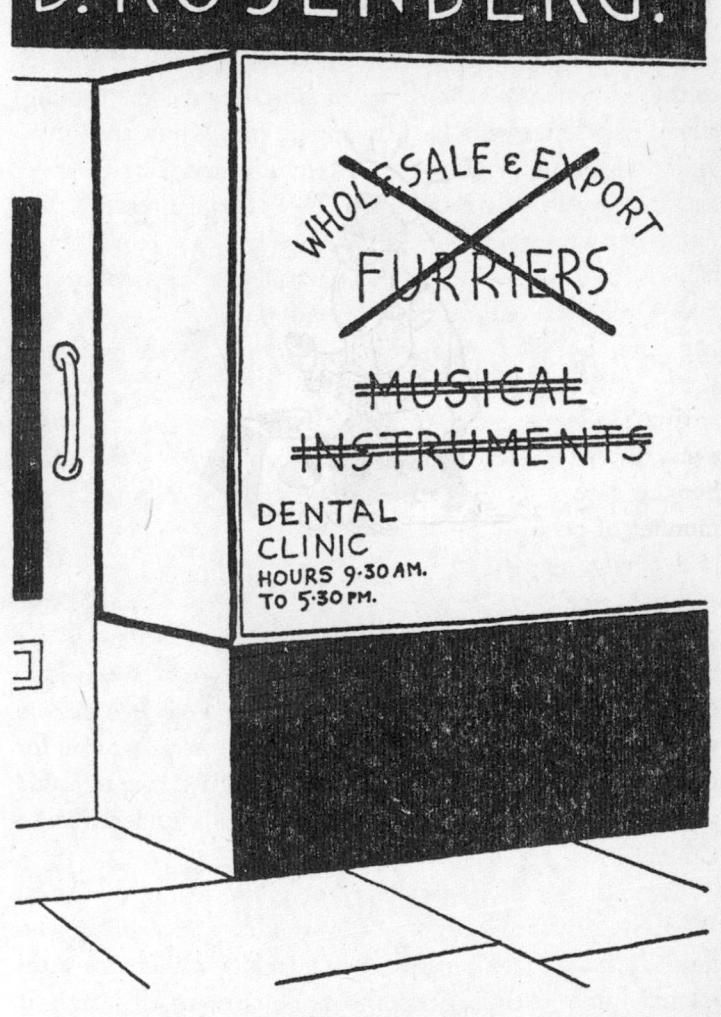

A Rosenberg by any other name . . .

roads of unlimited possibility, and the amazing career of the youthful multi-millionaire who starts his life as a newspaper magnate or refrigerator king and ends it as a good, wise, elderly boot-black—has still to be recorded.

IT is great fun dying in the United States of America. It is great fun first of all for the undertakers who make a wonderful living out of it but also for the deceased who suddenly becomes the centre of attention and fuss.

American newspapers are full of funeral advertisements:

'Funeral Service that will leave your mind at ease for ever.' Or:

'A Funeral Service you will really enjoy.' Or:

'Dignified funeral.' Or:

'Comfortable funerals.' Or:

'Funeral that will make your family happy for months.' Or:

'Unforgettable funerals as low as $150. The same with southern plants $200. The same with two palms $215.' Or:

'Funerals with hidden neon lighting from Louis XIV rooms.' Or:

'Come to us! We'll bury you better!'

And people go. They discuss their own funerals with gusto, choose the coffin (first their measurements are taken for this purpose), choose the decorations on it, the songs to be sung, the palms to be exhibited, how they are going to be embalmed. They pay in instalments and look forward to the great day.

I do not wish to go into all the details of this morbid but flourishing industry although there is something fascinating in the gaiety of the undertakers. They are the only business-men in the world who can look upon everybody on earth as prospective customers. They look at old men with a reproachful eye and with sanctimoniously hidden self-assurance and, at the same time, one can see the hope shining in

'Why, Elmer, it's perfect!'

their eyes that they will order it with southern plants and two palms.

It is worth pointing out that dishwashing is not the only occupation a man without much skill and expert knowledge can undertake, when absolutely broke. You can always become a professional mourner. The undertaker will pay you 25 per cent and his price list is this:

> You stand by the coffin with head bent and looking very sad—five dollars.
>
> The same with occasional tears—ten dollars.
>
> The same with crying, shrieking and sobbing—twenty-five dollars.
>
> For seventy five dollars you have to throw yourself into the grave after the coffin.

Orders of this kind, however, have recently decreased. (Because the price is considered unreasonably high.)

ADVERTISEMENTS

I AM ready to bet that in your *naïveté* you believe that advertising is the art of convincing people of the remarkable qualities of your wares; of persuading them to prefer your product to any other make; and of keeping certain brands permanently in the public eye.

This is a misconception. Advertising—as I read somewhere—is the art of convincing people that they want certain things they do not want at all; of making them dissatisfied with everything they have; of making them thoroughly unhappy.

Advertisements in America are ubiquitous. They fill the newspapers and cover the walls, they are on menu cards and in your daily post, on pamphlets and on match boxes, they are shouted through loud speakers and shown in the cinemas, flashed electrically and written on the sky by aeroplanes and whispered in front of your window while you sleep so that you should dream of tooth paste, shoe polishes and soap flakes.

Leaving the problem of 'commercials'—i.e. the spoken and sung radio advertisements—for the moment, I find that there are five main ways of making people particularly unhappy.

(1) *Repetition.* If you hear these five letters: L.S.M.F.T. for the first time in your life, you remain cool and unimpressed. L.S.M.F.T. *Lucky Strike Means Fine Tobacco.* 'And what then?' you say. It is not funny, it is not witty, in fact, it is simple, silly and flat. Then you try to find the President's latest speech in the newspaper, but you cannot find it. You find these five letters instead: L.S.M.F.T. You travel on the subway and try to think of a killing reply to an important and annoying letter you have received but you cannot think of anything, because wherever you look you see only five letters: L.S.M.F.T. You take a walk in a dark street in comparative solitude, thinking of your beloved, and suddenly a neon advertisement flashes into your eyes: L.S.M.F.T. You want to write a poem on the uselessness and vanity of worldly pleasures but you only write down fifty times: *Lucky Strike Means Fine Tobacco*. If you try to recite the alphabet you are sure to slip up: g, h, i, j, k, l, s, m, f, t. . . . At this stage the advertisement has achieved its purpose. You will then and there take a solemn oath that whatever should happen in the future, however long you may live, you would rather go without smoking altogether than put one single Lucky Strike into your mouth.

(2) *Logical conclusions*. Advertisements have a special logic of their own. They tell you by implication that if you use a certain orange squeezer in your kitchen, you remain young, lovely and beautiful; if you wash with a certain soap you become rich; if you wear a certain type of underwear you inherit a large sum from a wealthy uncle and if you use only a special kind of tomato ketchup you learn foreign languages more easily. Of course, people are much too intelligent to believe such silly statements. But as after all there may be *something* in it—why not try? And as people who inherit large sums from wealthy uncles usually do wear some type of underwear and a few others who insist on a certain kind of tomato ketchup do learn French with the greatest ease, the proof is soon to be found that the advertisements—amazing as it may seem —spoke the golden truth.

Inheritance

(3) *The semi-scientific approach.* The word: 'scientific' has a magic effect in America. You may put up a notice: 'Scalp massage': this is quite ineffective. But if you say: 'Scientific scalp massage'—that is a different matter. After all, the least you can expect is that your scalp should be massaged by a scientist. A shoe polish manufacturer invented the verb: *to lanolize.* Other shoe polishes just clean your shoes—nicely, cleanly, efficiently—but E. shoe polish lanolizes them. The word has no meaning whatever but it is quite obvious that everybody would much rather have his shoes lanolized than merely cleaned. I am a rather lazy shoe lanolizer but I just could not resist the temptation. If you have 50,000 dollars to spend, you can persuade people that while other tooth pastes just clean their teeth, Atlantis tooth paste saturnizes them; that any other soap just washes their clothes but Atlantis soap kepplerizes them. And all good people in America would much rather spend their time lanolizing, saturnizing, kepplerizing, constricating, saharizing, tripodizing and patagonizing than washing and cleaning, because washing and cleaning, after all, *are* rather dull.

The other approach on the same line is to give people statistics. You state, for instance, that Amalda floor polish gives 42 per cent more shine to the floor with 37 per cent less effort than any other make. If anybody questions your statement and declares that its stupidity is too obvious for any child over the age of four, you smile in a superior way and explain to him that this has been 'scientifically' proved. If he is still unconvinced, tell him that the real explanation lies in the fact that any other floor polish just cleans the floor but Amalda platonizes it.

(4) *Glorify your weakness.* There was a chewing-gum firm in New York which used only artificial flavours instead of real fruit flavours. This fact became known to the public and sales dropped off. Then suddenly huge advertisements appeared: 'X—the only chewing-gum made with real ARTIFICIAL flavor.'* People's imagination was caught and few would look at any other chewing-gum now.

(5) *Religion.* Religion has recently become extremely popular. In the advertising field, I mean. Churches advertise, too, ('Come to us and you will be not only saved but amnetized!') but this is not the real point. Religion has immense possibilities. I print here a little article, published in one of the American newspapers while I was over there. No comment is needed, I believe:

> Last week company-president Maurice C. Smith Jr hired the Reverend Dale D. Dutton away from a wealthy Baptist Church to make him Bristol Shoe's vice-president of Christian relations. The job: 'To do good as he is led to do it.' The budget: $100,000 p.a. The inspiration: 'His instructions will come not from the company but from God. . . . We do not expect to sell any more shoes because of this venture.'

If the sales fall off, spend more money on advertising. But beware of one thing: do *not* improve the quality of

* They really mean flavour

your goods. That will leave you a smaller sum to spend on advertising—and then you are lanolized. Maybe you are lanolized for good.

'EVERY country has the radio service it deserves.' To apply this axiom to the United States of America would be a grave insult and I hasten to add that the United States deserve something much better than the radio service it has. American radio is the reverse of the Shakespearean stage. In Shakespeare's time the world's greatest dramas were acted with the most primitive technical arrangements; on the American air the world's most primitive writing is performed under perfect technical conditions.

There are four major radio networks: ABC (American Broadcasting Corporation, four stations and 215 affiliated stations); CBS (Columbia Broadcasting System, seven stations, 157 affiliated stations and 123 Latin American stations); MBS (Mutual Broadcasting System, 329 affiliated stations); and NBC (National Broadcasting Company, six stations, 153 affiliated stations and 162 Latin American stations). In addition to the network there are innumerable local stations—broadcasting in many languages but mostly in English—and a number of them are very important and influential. A local New York, Chicago or Los Angeles station, after all, has several million potential listeners.

Licences for broadcasting stations (for receivers no licences are needed) are issued by the Federal Communications Commission which body is supposed to coordinate and, to some extent, control the work of all stations. Some time ago FCC sharply criticised the 'broadcast licensees' and the result was a tremendous uproar on the licensees' part because they considered that 'freedom of speech' was endangered. Whenever a big commercial trust is criticised or its rights curtailed it cries out that some fundamental human right is in peril.

The main features of American broadcasting are these:

(1) Radio is a permanent background noise in America. All the radios of the land seem to be switched on all the time, and considering that 34·6 per cent of the population own radio sets compared with 18·8 per cent in the United Kingdom, you may guess that they are capable of a considerable din. In apartments, in the street, in shops, restaurants, cars and taxis, any-where and everywhere the noise goes on—it is your fate to listen to it, whether you like it or hate it.

(2) Public opinion, taste and culture are led and directed by laxative, cigarette, soap and cheese com-panies. They buy a certain amount of time on the radio, during which they try to convince you that *their* laxative is tastier, more efficient, cheaper and more beautiful to look at than any other laxative in the world. To fill up time between two commercials, they hire some comedians who crack a number of stale jokes and laugh at them themselves, loudly and heartily. Of course, Mr Bob Hope or Mr Morgan and a few others *are* funny and amuse you most of the time, but they are very rare exceptions.

This system was hailed as the real freedom. No state control, they boasted, no censorship. Some keen observers, however, noticed after the lapse of a few years that the real aim of laxative firms was not to raise the cultural standard of the nation but to sell more laxatives to people whether they needed them or not. In this they have succeeded; and the result is American broadcasting.

(3) Everybody and everything is 'Hooperated'. All radio performers and writers depend on Mr C. E.

"...besides, Camellia cigarettes increase your height..."

Believe it or not

Hooper's fortnightly *Hooper Ratings*. Hooper speaks on behalf of thirty five million American radio families, makes $1,000,000 p.a. and has nearly two thousand employees who ring up people, trying to find out what they listen to. Mr Hooper tells in his *Ratings* what per cent of radio fans listen to a certain programme. America is a scientific country. Mr Hooper's assistants ring up people day and night, collect answers to relevant and irrelevant questions put in a skilful or clumsy way, issue statistics by the score and state extremely scientifically indeed that a song called *Open the Door Richard* is 137 times more popular than Beethoven's *Fifth Symphony* and Mr Ovington's chats on 'How I like my cheese and why' are 217·08 times better liked than *A Midsummer Night's Dream*.

(4) A special feature in American broadcasting is the soap opera. Once upon a time, very few people listened in around noon and then a soap company hit on the idea that special broadcasts should be initiated for women who are at home preparing lunch. So the soap operas started their career and now practically all stations broadcast these soap operas between 12 noon and 4 P.M. on every weekday from Monday to Friday. They last fifteen minutes each. One of the most popular is the *Romance of Helen Trent*. Miss Trent is just an average American girl. She has been thirty two for the last two decades; she is intelligent, beautiful and employed as a designer by one of the Hollywood film companies and in spite of the fact that she is begged and besought twice every week to become a film star she refuses and remains just that little, unassuming average American girl she has never been.

She solves life's problems for anyone who happens to come near her or pass down the street in front of her window. These are usually grave and momentous problems. There is for example a young man who has charming manners and an admirable character, is a graduate of Princeton University, has an income of four million dollars per year, loves Helen Trent's colleague madly; she loves him, too, and their parents agree to the marriage—what are they to do? Everybody is at a loss until Helen, with a few simple, calm, wise words arranges their lives and separates them for ever.

Or there is another feature: *My gal Sunday*. This gal Sunday is a Midwesterner, born on a Sunday and much later married to an English lord, a certain Lord Henry (Henry being his Christian name). The problem is: can the little Midwestern gal be happy with the rich English lord? They have lived together for twelve years, have innumerable children, I believe, but the problem is still unsolved. Lord Henry gets into trouble every week; all his friends are murdered, he is always suspected of killing them off but in the last moment his innocence is always proved and Lord Henry returns from jail to his beloved Sunday, spends a quiet week-end with her and next Monday commits a new murder. Few members of the British aristocracy spend so much time in jail as Lord Henry. Little wonder he can never spare a minute to drop into the House of Lords to take part in a Foreign Affairs debate.

(5) Quiz programmes are popular, too. A few members of the audience make fools of themselves in one way or another and in return they receive prizes.

And what prizes! Whenever you see a person carrying a refrigerator or a piano on his back or leading a camel through the streets of New York, you may rest assured that he has just won a quiz prize. Here is a notice I copied out from a New York paper:

Mrs William H. MacC. of Lock Haven, Pa, won $17,590 in prizes on Saturday night by correctly identifying Clara Bow, one time screen 'it' girl, as the mysterious 'Mrs Hush' on NBC's *Truth or Consequences* programme. The solver of the eight-week-old radio mystery won an airplane, an automobile, a week-end in New York, a week's vacation in Idaho, a year's maid service, a completely equipped trailer and a coat of paint, inside and out, for her house.

(6) There are some excellent and intelligent radio-commentators on the air. They are brave and candid and give balanced views on world events. One of these, in spite of the fact that his *Hooper Ratings* were the highest among all commentators and even higher than a great number of musical shows, was taken off the air by a commercial firm because of his mildly leftish tendencies. To use the immense cultural possibilities of radio mainly for the purpose of persuading people to buy more shirts, canned fruit, laxatives and boot polish is 'freedom of speech'; to take a brilliant commentator off the air because he says what he believes to be the truth is 'freedom of private enterprise'.

(7) But the main features are, of course, the commercials. They are declaimed in prose and recited in verse, sung by soloists and choirs, persuading, cajoling, threatening, warning and ordering people to buy X underwear or Y tinned beans. Every performance, except the sacred baseball match commentaries, is interrupted to tell you that you will become ravishingly beautiful if you eat Z cheese or else that you are sure to die young, poor and neglected if you do not use U shoe polish. One advertisement tells you in effect, that if you use a certain perfume, you become so irresistibly desirable that people will rape you in Fifth Avenue. You are told that honest men use only Akropolis fountain pens and a minute later that no decent person would touch anything but Muse fountain pens. One Texas radio station carried 2,215 commercials in 133 broadcasting hours, an average of 16·7 per hour. Once during a performance of *King Lear*, the tragedy flowed on in its majesty until at its climax King Lear broke loose in a ferocious malediction, condemning all his daughters for not drinking 'Optimus' orange juice for breakfast.

In short, the basic principles of broadcasting are these:

The main cultural aim is to sell more cheese to the public than it can consume.

Freedom of speech means freedom of great commercial firms to pull down all the rest of the people to their own intellectual level.

News is free; commercials are sacred.

'And get this: wear a "Trufit" truss, or else—!'

I ALWAYS felt slightly insulted when I bought a news-paper in America. For three or four cents (there *The Times* is cheaper than any other paper) the newsvendor handed over a bulky volume of about eighty pages and I hadn't the slightest hope of reading more of it than the headlines and a few paragraphs here and there. What would you feel if on entering a restaurant and ordering roast beef, the waiters were to bring you three whole oxen with half a ton of Idaho potatoes (an Idaho potato is as large as a sizable marrow), or if you asked for a Frankfurter and six waiters dragged up a fourteen-yard long pole of meat and placed an ancient yataghan and a pitchfork beside your plate? I always felt just as you would feel in such a case whenever I received the usual overdose of my morning paper. I had to read it in a hurry, almost in a panic, because the evening papers are published early and if one loses any precious time, one can never catch up with it again. A friend of mine, a visitor from Tahiti, once remarked to me:

'In a month's time I'll go back to Tahiti. There, you know, we have a two-page news sheet published daily. It gives only the gist of world events and each item consists of two or three lines. No baseball, no sensational licence cases, no boxing matches, no murder stories and no twelve column reports on unimportant speeches by unimportant politicians. Just the gist of the news, fairly balanced and written in a rather dull manner, with the aloofness of a detached observer. I'll go back to Tahiti and there I shall know once again what is happening in New York.'

As far as I could make out, in America nobody reads political news in any case. Women read the advertisements only; schoolchildren the comic strips, also called—for some unknown reason—the 'funnies'; well-dressed people read the sports news and people in rags read only the stock exchange report. (Or, may be, *vice versa*: people who read the stock exchange reports only, are always clad in rags.)

Apart from the size, American papers differ but little from the newspapers of other lands. On the whole, perhaps, they are better informed and not quite as carefully written as . . . well, offhand I can think of only ten newspapers in the whole world which are really carefully written. American papers have correspondents in every important city of the world and every correspondent is anxious to make a scoop. Consequently they telegraph or telephone home the 'real background' of and the 'inside information' on all past and future political events—full of the 'human touch'—and cases have definitely been registered in the annals of journalism when these inside stories were closely related to the truth.

I should like to enumerate a few points which struck me:

(1) There are no national dailies in the United States. Distances are too vast for any paper to cover the whole country. Magazines, on the other hand, can cover the whole national market and their circulation runs into astronomical figures. Well, magazines are magazines. But there is a special kind of American magazine—the *New Yorker* is the prototype—written by grown ups for grown ups, with witty cartoons, amusing stories and biting comments on current events. I believe that England would do well with such a periodical. I do not wish to hurt the feelings of *Punch* which *is* brilliantly written and always on a high level; but I feel the time has come when somebody should tell the editor that Lord Beaconsfield is no longer in office and tactfully inform him of the regrettable death of Queen Victoria.

(2) The digests are in a category of their own. The *Reader's Digest* is almost compulsory for everyone. Its sale exceeds thirteen million copies monthly, not counting the numerous foreign editions and the editions for the blind, the deaf and the illiterate. *Reader's Digest* is, after the Bible, the most widely circulated publication in the world.

People, after all, have little time to read and when they read these digests, they have the feeling of having read everything worth looking into. There is no subject the *Reader's Digest* will not touch, from baseball to religion, from cancer to dancing, from the art of happiness to the life of a salmon and from the higher education of the silk-worm to the hair-net industry in North China. All its articles are 'condensed' from some other newspaper or periodical, and the reader consequently gets everything in a dehydrated form— skinned, stoned and castrated. He only has to put these articles into a glass of water and when they are dissolved, drink them quickly and he gets a dose of culture. Many articles are ordered by the *Reader's Digest*, edited by its numerous editors (the periodical has about three editors for each article published) and printed in a satellite paper from which the *Digest* then reprints them in a condensed form. Occasionally these 'planted' articles are condensed in such a way that they are considerably longer than the article they are condensed from and it also happens occasionally that the 'reprint' appears a few days before the original.

'Dizzy's got the push!'

There are other popular digests in America—but of course, nothing to compare with the *Reader's Digest*. There are digests to deal with every subject under the sun—sport, agricultural, movie, international, Wild West, Negro and music digests—and it is little wonder that a business man I met was seriously considering publishing a *Digest of Digests* condensing all the condensed articles.

(3) In the last few years breasts have been discovered in America in general and in the American press in particular. I mean, the fact has been noticed by some journalists (nothing can remain hidden from these people) that women have breasts, usually two per woman. A young lady has become a Hollywood star mainly because she succeeded in securing more than her fair share in breasts. Many New York papers describe women in this way: 'The name of the young lady is Miss Eleanor W., aged 21, hair brown, height 5' 4", bust 34".' Reading these New York papers carefully you may improve your historical knowledge considerably and usefully as you learn the bust measurement of every woman from Sarah (Mrs Abraham) to Mme Tojo.

(4) The last phenomenon I wish to mention is the comic strips. They are called comic strips because they are neither comic nor strips. Just as a foreigner, coming to England, takes years to understand the British passion for queueing or tepid beer or the fact that a strongly Conservative newspaper can allow a left wing cartoonist to attack the paper's and its proprietor's policy in its own columns—so no visitor in the United States can understand the fascination and magic of these comic strips for so many millions. With the single exception of the *New York Times* no New York daily can forgo the comics, including the high ranking *New York Herald Tribune* and the ambitious *P.M.* The dailies run the comics in instalments, some giving two, three or four pages to them. On Sundays they are printed in colour and the coloured sheets are taken out of their usual place and put right on top of the front page, because, after all, it is the comics that sell the paper.

Once a stationer asked me in astonishment:

'What do you say? There are no comics in England?'

'That's what I said.'

'Good Heavens! How can they sell the papers then?'

I could not answer his query but after this conversation I spent a very uneasy night dreaming of *The Times*, the *Manchester Guardian* and the *Daily Telegraph* full of comic strips.

Some of the comics relate the adventures of various supermen who dress like athletes or circus acrobats. (This does not, apparently, cause the slightest surprise in Fifth Avenue.) They beat up everybody, knock out former boxing champions, solve all the riddles of the universe, defend the innocent and punish the guilty. Others tell the story of little girls or fairies, others of Texan cowboys, young suffering maidens, sportsmen, criminals, jockeys, master detectives and master killers. People keep talking in these strips, a flood of conversation bubbles out of their mouths and they put their deep problems in a very cute and brilliantly intelligent way, such as (I quote verbatim):

A man is unfair to himself, don't you agree, when he shows dumb loyalty to a girl he merely thinks he loves . . . when he knows that *another* girl, one who has *just come into his life* perhaps, is the girl he *really* loves? [Italics from the original.]

Whenever I discussed the problems of these strips, I was told by newspapermen and others that they have an immense educational value. If they alluded to the fact that they teach people good ju-jitsu tricks, marvellous ways to set houses on fire and how to steal

horses in Texas, I see their point. Otherwise I do not, but I take their word for it.

However much I write about comics, it will not convey a clear picture to the reader who is not familiar with the subject. I think an example is necessary, so the two authors of this book will try to give you one illustrating the nature and, at the same time, the immense educational value of the comics. Here we give you the chapter on Pythagoras from Mr Bertrand Russell's book *A History of Western Philosophy*:

III. BLACK AND WHITE

'FOR WHITES ONLY'

DEMOCRACY is a reality in America. It is, however, like a beautiful woman with a long, crooked nose or with a few teeth missing. It is democracy with a hitch. The Negroes are the black spot of America.

The world is a wicked place and the poor Americans are so busy defending the rights of Hindus in Pakistan, Moslems in India, Jews in Palestine, Koreans in Japan, Italians in Yugoslavia and Hungarians in Czechoslovakia that they simply cannot give a thought to Negroes in the United States.

There are well over twelve million Negroes in the U.S. —that is, more than the whole population of Canada. Almost ten million of them live in the so-called Southern States, which are, roughly speaking, the South-Eastern States. On the other hand, there are seven states where the number of Negroes is under one thousand. Now, obviously, the Southerners are the great experts on the Negro problem and they will explain to you that the crimes of Negroes are terrible and manifold and their persecution justified.

(1) First of all, the Negro is black. This seems to be one of his main crimes and is held very much against him. A great number of Southerners would be much more tolerant with the Negro, if only he were not black. When discussing the Negro question with white

Southerners, I heard the horrified remark innumerable times:

'But don't you see, they are black!'

I must admit there is a great deal of truth in this very able observation: the Negroes *are* black—no use denying it.

(2) They are illiterate or at least uneducated. I believe this second charge is slightly old-fashioned and should be replaced by a new one. It is a very old recipe to exclude people from schools or keep them in the utmost poverty so that they should be unable to go to school and then accuse them of being uneducated.

(3) They are over-ambitious and pushing—they learn too much.

(4) They are full of racial prejudice. Millions of them are satisfied with their situation, they believe in their own inferiority and have a strong dislike of Negroes coming from the North and talking about a real abolition of slavery. I should go so far as to state that some of them even like being lynched. Not all of them and not all the time—just a few Negroes, every now and then, let us say twice a year, in the height of the season.

(5) They do not 'keep in their place'. So-called fair-minded Southerners told me that they have nothing against those Negroes who know their place, they only object to the 'uppity' ones. In other words they are perfectly adorable as long as they remain servants, janitors, waiters, sewage cleaners, boot-blacks, unskilled manual workers (preferably receiving very low wages). The trouble starts only when they talk of freedom and equality and other outrageous things of

The position of the Negro in American society

this nature and do not honour their white masters (in many cases illiterate, bad-mannered, white coolies).

(6) They stink. Negroes—mostly those who do not wash for several weeks on end—have a peculiar smell of their own. I met a great number of white Southerners who were too busy to spend much time in washing and I dare say I could tell them without difficulty from a rose in full bloom.

(7) Their fathers were slaves. Note: this is the shame of the Negroes and not of their masters.

(8) They have criminal tendencies. There are indeed some ugly crimes—lynching for instance—in which Negroes are involved without fail, in one way or another.

These are the crimes the Negroes are charged with. Yes, their persecution *would* be justified but, of course, there is no persecution at all. The Fifteenth Amendment of the Constitution declares:

> The right of the citizens of the United States to vote shall not be denied or abridged by the United States or by any State on account of race, color, or previous condition of servitude.

This rule is scrupulously adhered to and Negroes are not deprived of their franchise on account of their race and colour but they are deprived of it by the use of various devices such as the poll tax and white primary laws.

Then there is segregation in the South but the principle is: separate but equal. In buses for instance the front places are reserved for white men, that is true, but on the other hand, the back places are reserved for Negroes. (Should you sit among Negroes, the driver will refuse to start.) On every train there are Jim Crow cars—cars reserved for Negroes—usually just behind the engine so that they should get a fair amount of smoke, while the rest of the train is reserved for white passengers. If Negroes are crowded together in a dangerous and unhealthy way while each white passenger has seven seats for himself, that is just bad luck, but they will not change the arrangements. It is true that Negroes are excluded from restaurants, hotels, cinemas, theatres, hospitals and many other public places, but, in turn, white men do not frequent Negro establishments. Negroes are excluded from many shops and even when the white owner graciously condescends to accept their money, he forbids them to try on hats, suits and gloves in many States. Negroes cannot get into a restaurant car, or book a place in a sleeper or in a pullman car but they are fully entitled to stay out. It is easy to see that these arrangements are just and fair, worthy of the defendants of all minorities, provided the minorities are far away, in other people's countries. Separate and equal: all Negroes are quite separate and all Negroes are equal.

The real issue is, as many people explained it to me, the freedom of the whites. They must be free to have parks, hospitals, libraries for whites only, provided that other equally good parks etc are reserved for negroes, too. If you ask Southerners whether Negroes do have equally good parks, libraries and hospitals, they will laugh their heads off as this is considered a capital joke. White people must be free to keep Negroes out of their own restaurants by various devices and now, at last, they have received the legal right of lynching, too. Until now, there was some doubt in many

'It is your duty, gentlemen, to reach a verdict simply and solely according to the evidence that is put before you, to banish from your minds all consideration of extraneous circumstances, to preserve complete and absolute impartiality, to uphold without fear or favor the integrity of the Law and the sacred right of every citizen of the United States—the right to a FAIR TRIAL. While there is nothing in our Constitution against the acquittal of a negro . . .'

white minds as to whether lynching was really lawful. In May 1947 twenty eight white men were indicted and tried (for the first time in the history of the South) for lynching a Negro youth. Sixteen persons out of twenty eight had admitted in signed statements that they had taken part in the lynching, but an all-white jury acquitted all the defendants on every one of the ninety eight charges. They returned their verdict in five and a half hours—giving about three and a half minutes to each count. The jury, of course, was supposed to decide a question of fact only, but the South interpreted this verdict as a general permit for lynching and a few hours later another Negro was duly lynched by a white mob.

The North is a Paradise, compared with the South. There are no Jim Crow cars there, Negroes have the right to vote and often are employed together with white people, doing the same jobs. But they are unable to get an apartment any-where except in Harlem (though a negligible number live in Brooklyn, in the Bronx and Greenwich Village). They have to pay exorbitant prices in overcrowded slums, they cannot hire rooms in hotels and they are excluded from most of the restaurants and many other public places—although, every now and then, the managers of hotels and restaurants are fined for excluding them. Whenever I went out to have lunch or dinner with a Negro, I had to ask him to choose a place and even so, many inquisitive or hostile looks were thrown at us. Even the workers follow suit. While C.I.O. specifically forbids discrimination, there are a great number of American Federation of Labour Unions which exclude Negroes by provision of their Con-stitution, others which exclude them by tacit consent and others again which afford them only segregated auxiliary status.

The law may say whatever it likes; a few high-minded judges may pronounce judgments inspired by the noblest sentiments; a gradually enlightened and increasingly worried public opinion may try to exercise pressure, but the wall of prejudice seems to be impenetrable. The owner of a restaurant will say to a Negro that all his tables are booked; or if a Negro succeeds in finding a place he will instruct his waiters not to serve him. Then the owner withdraws into a corner and continues a heated argument with his friends about the problem of the Macedonian minority not enjoying equal rights in Bulgaria or the Jews not being fairly treated in Palestine. Should he allow Negroes to eat at his place, he would lose many white clients; should the owner of a house let apartments to Negroes, the price of his estate— and all estates in the neighbourhood—would fall. Should such a danger arise, all estate agents would appeal to the racial pride of the public, organise demonstrations and shout high-minded slogans to save the estate prices. It is true that this treatment of the Negro is against the spirit and the letter of the Constitution and it is true that the Constitution is sacred. But the Dollar is more sacred. High should be our reverence for the Constitution; but estate prices should be higher.

During the war, Negroes were allowed to serve in the United States armed forces but segregation was fully enforced. The Negroes served in separate units and lived in separate barracks. Apart from minor details, the only major exception from the segregation rules was that German and Japanese bullets were not marked: 'For Whites Only.'

Prejudices cut too deep—many people say—and there is no solution. I believe there *is* a solution. As soon as the presence of Negroes increases estate prices instead of lowering them, all the walls of segregation will fall down.

IF you walk around in Harlem—in the black Metropolis, or leaving euphemism apart for a moment, in the black ghetto of New York—you can see an interesting and much-discussed racial problem reflected in the windows of beauty parlours and women's shops. You will see all kinds of dummies, just as in the windows of similar establishments all the world over. But *these* dummies are black. Black-faced dummies with wiry and sometimes curly hair proclaim the skill of the hairdresser or dressmaker. Then you notice a great number of shops with white dummies only; then some with creole dummies; and then again other windows where black dummies are carefully mixed with white ones.

Negroes cannot quite decide whether they should be dark or light. Race conscious people are proud of being dark and look down upon the lighter ones, who obviously have some white blood—and this is, in fact, the truth in the case of two thirds of Harlem's inhabitants. Others, on the other hand, look down upon the dark ones and would do anything in their power to lighten their skins. Negro newspapers preach racial consciousness but at the same time are compelled to advertise ointments which are supposed to make one's skin lighter.

Harlem is the black variation of New York. The Negroes are Americans first and Negroes only in the second place.

Snobbery is a complicated enough business, as it is, for white Americans. But it is child's play compared with the task facing a dark-skinned snob.

If you are a Negro and wish to be a snob, you have to distinguish between extra-racial and intra-racial snobbery. Extra-racial snobbery is, of course, a natural and probably quite justified reaction to being persecuted and oppressed. If you want to be a proper Negro in New York, you must

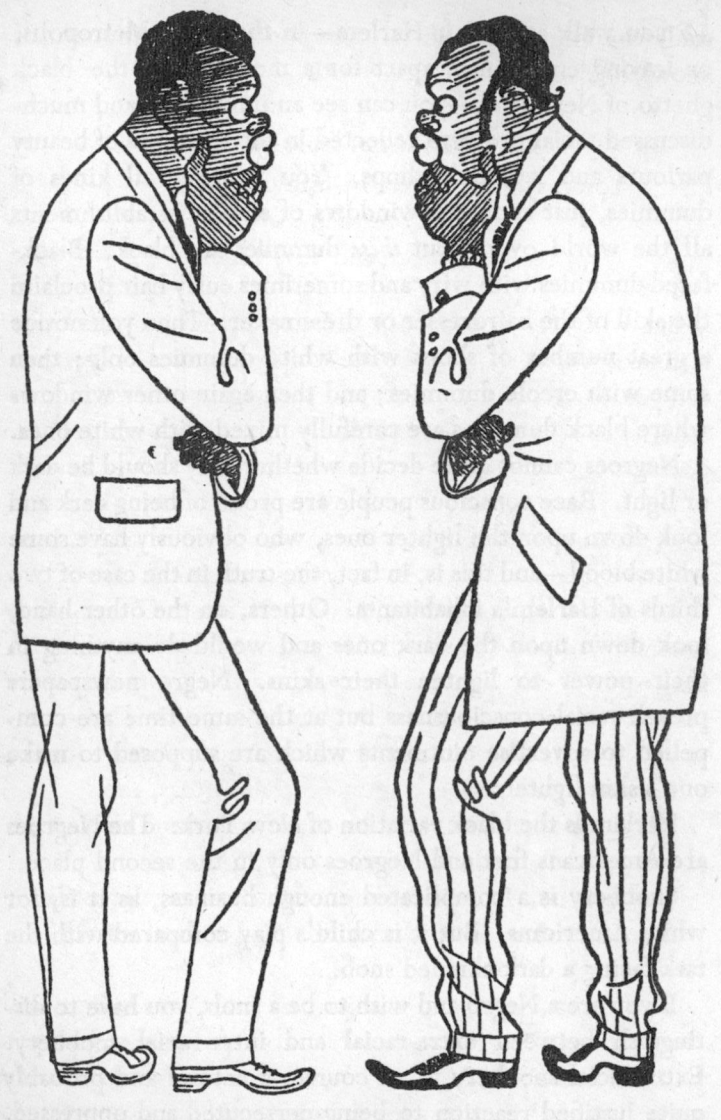

To be or not to be . . .

study the following rules as they contain the minimum of knowledge you can get along with.

Extra-racial snobbery

You may (*a*) hate all white people,
(*b*) ignore them, or
(*c*) adore and envy them.

But whatever you choose, imitate them. Imitate their manners, smoke their long cigars, wear their red-and-green-and-golden ties and even understand their anti-Negro attitude, at least, against certain classes or groups of the Negro population.

Once I was taken by a white lady friend of mine to a Negro club for backward youths where a boy of fourteen acquainted us with his racial theories and plans:

'One day we are going into the streets,' he said in a dreaming voice—'We shall carry long, long knives, dripping with blood. We are going to kill all the white people on that night. All of them. You too, Miss Catherine, although you are very nice and sweet to us.' Then he looked at me and added politely: 'And all the visitors, too.'

'How can you say things like that?' my friend exclaimed, surprised and a little terrified.

The boy looked at us and replied with an angelic smile:

'I am so young, Miss Catherine. And so backward.'

You must oppose all inter-racial marriages. You will come across very few of those, at any rate. Sometimes you will find brave people, Negro men and white women or vice versa, who fall in love with each other and are prepared to defy all racial barriers. Fairly often, you will see a poor

white girl who sells herself to a rich Negro. The marriage
of a white man to a Negro girl is a much rarer occurrence.
Whatever the reason for the marriage, the white partner
becomes a Negro in the eyes of the white community
and all his or her children are considered Negroes. He
remains however the white stranger and intruder in the
eyes of the Negroes. They take up a 'we are not honoured'
attitude. I personally consider this attitude ignoble, mean
and revengeful, but, good Heavens, would I share it if I
were a Negro!

Apart from having a general attitude to whites, you may
despise certain groups. The nineteenth century British
antagonism to the Irish, for instance, still survives in Black
New England and beyond its boundaries. Nowadays, however, it is much more fashionable to be an anti-Semite.
Harlem's white shop keepers and landlords are said to be
mostly Jews and they are not hated as white men or as shopkeepers and landlords, but as Jews.

The story goes around in New York that a very black
Negro woman tried on a hat with a lot of fruit and flowers
and other decorations on it, looked at herself in the mirror
and, horrified, exclaimed:

'My goodness, don't I look Jewish!'

Intra-racial snobbery

The doctrine of intra-racial snobbery is much more
difficult to absorb.

First of all there is the difference in money, culture and
profession. The dividing line between rich and poor seems
to be much stronger than all racial bonds.

The Negroes of lighter shade look down upon very dark
Negroes.

Very dark Negroes look down upon lighter ones—in this connection you must remember that there is no shade between pitch-black and light creole, mixed with yellow, red and even green that is not represented in Harlem. Real, full-blooded African Negroes who migrated recently into the United States from Nigeria, the Gold Coast, Congo, Liberia and similar countries or colonies, look down upon all American Negroes, because they consider themselves the aristocracy of the race and, in fact, you can find some Negro princes in their ranks.

Then there are all the Negro emigrants and refugees. After all, America is such a rich and generous mother that even her step-sons can live a better and fuller life than many of them could in their country of origin. One quarter of Harlem's population forms Black New England. The Black New Englanders are proud Britishers who resent racial discrimination, which they hardly knew (except the Jamaicans), keep their British nationality, celebrate whenever some joyful event occurs in the British royal family, speak a kind of Americanised and colonised cockney, play a large and important part in Harlem's cultural life, smile at everybody and are jeered at by everybody else.

There are the Haitians who come from an independent Negro republic, where white men are a tolerated minority but treated in a much nobler fashion than Negroes are usually treated by white men.

There are the Spanish-speaking coloured men, chiefly the Puerto Ricans, who suffer discrimination from the whites and try to keep the balance by discriminating against the Negroes.

There are the French-speaking Negroes, who arrived from various French possessions, mix much more freely

The position of the American in Haitian society

with white Frenchmen than any other group in the community mixes with any white group and celebrate the anniversary of the fall of the Bastille every year.

Then there are the Moslem Negroes and the half-caste Negro-Indians, Negro-Chinese, Negro-Filipino and Negro-Malayan mixtures and finally, among other millions of native American Negroes, the ancient tribe of Negro Jews, about ten thousand of them, who have practised Judaism for thousands of years, read the *Talmud Torah*, send their children to *Yeshivos*, eat *kosher* dishes only, do not work on Saturdays, faithfully follow their bearded rabbi and are very clever in business. A number of them speak Yiddish only. Some people believe that it is a slight exaggeration to be a Negro and a Jew rolled into one and suggest that they should choose: either-or. The Negro Jews are not the Jews of the Negro community, in the European sense of the word, but they are clannish themselves, and do not call themselves Negroes, but Ethiopians or Afro-Americans or Isro-Africans.

This classification is, of course, over-simplified. There are very many Negroes who bear their hard lot with much courage and intelligence. Basically, however, there is a great deal of truth in my classification. I believe, that if the Negroes were not snobs, discrimination against them would be justified; things as they are only prove that the Negroes are not better or worse than the rest of the community or than the rest of us.

IV. MILD AND BITTER

THE STATES OF THE UNION

NINE years ago, soon after my arrival in England, a friend of mine invited me to an international football match. 'International?' I asked him. 'Against whom? France?' 'Oh no,' he replied, 'that wouldn't be interesting. Wales.' I was very much surprised to hear that an English-Welsh match was called an 'international'. My English friends, to whom I told this 'story', did not quite see what I was talking about. By now, of course, I know very well what all Continentals are apt to forget, that Great Britain is inhabited by three nations.

Most British, in the same way, are inclined to forget that the United States is not one huge country, but in fact, a federation of forty eight states. In addition to the forty eight states there is District of Columbia, better known as Washington D.C.

Some of the states detest one another wholeheartedly. A New Jersey man once explained to me what a pity it was they could not ally themselves with Connecticut and invade New York.

'What a shame,' I said sympathetically, 'that you haven't an army.'

'Why,' he replied, 'of course our state has its own militia.'

In some states you will find an over-developed local patriotism. The inhabitants of Texas are very nationalistic indeed. A number of Texas soldiers took part, for instance, in the invasion of France in 1944, whereupon one of the Texan papers came out with the headlines: 'TEXANS

INVADE NORMANDY'. There is a great antipathy between South and North and some Southerners still believe that the North treats them as a defeated nation and exploits them as a market; on the other hand Northerners—the Yankees—believe that the South should treat the Negroes better. People, who to my ear had exactly the same accent, jeer at one another because of their pronunciation.

In a recent book, edited by Dick Hyman and entitled *Looney Laws*, certain regulations, still in force in various states are collected and I should like to mention a few examples.

Some laws to maintain public decency

In Minnesota men's and women's underwear must not hang on the same clothes line.

In Elkhart, Indiana, there is a law against barbers threatening to cut off children's ears.

In St Joseph, Missouri, city firemen must not walk about in their underwear.

In Gary, Indiana, it is against the law to ride in a tramway within four hours of eating garlic.

In Monrie, Utah, it is illegal to dance with a girl unless daylight can be seen between you.

In Indiana it is forbidden to seduce a young lady while teaching her to roller skate.

For the defence of animals

In Maine it is against the law to set fire to a mule.

In Baltimore, Maryland, it is a penal offence to torture an oyster.

In Kentucky the shooting of clay pigeons during the breeding season is prohibited.

Strictly legal

In Alabama, if you have not been a resident for a year, you can be jailed for having salt water shrimps in your possession.

In California it is a penal offence to set a trap for mice unless you have a hunting licence.

In Seattle, Washington, goldfish must not ride in city buses unless they lie still.

In Louisville, Kentucky, it is prohibited to shoot fish with a bow and arrow.

In Joliet, Illinois, a woman can be jailed for trying on more than six garments in one shop.

Miscellaneous

In Sault Ste Marie, Michigan, it is a misdemeanour to spit against the wind.

In Kentucky no woman may appear in a bathing suit unless armed with a club.

In Arkansas, it is illegal to mispronounce the name of Arkansas. (By the way, for your convenience, it is pronounced: Ahr-kan-saw.)

In Mohave, Arizona, anyone caught stealing soap, must wash himself with it until all the soap is used up.

In Jonesboro, Georgia, it is against the law to say: 'Oh Boy!'

Public safety

In Fort Madison, Iowa, the fire department must practise for fifteen minutes before going to extinguish a fire.

Traffic law

In New Hampshire 'when two motor vehicles meet at an intersection, each shall come to a full stop and neither shall proceed until the other has gone.'

It would be easy to elaborate on this subject and make fun of the diversity of laws, regulations and customs in the various American states. The fact, however, that these American states succeeded in abolishing all possibility of going to war with one another and in establishing a great union is a tremendous achievement and an example for the whole world, especially for the United Nations. It was not such a very long time ago that people were declaring that to imagine that the various North American States could live under the same government was a naïve and utopian dream; just as people say today that it is a naïve and utopian dream that Soviet Russia and Peru, for instance, should obey the same central authority. The very existence of the United States, like that of the British Commonwealth of Nations, is a proof of great wisdom, toleration and states-manship. My above-quoted New Jersey friend, however, once remarked:

'It is easy for the British to live together in peace. Australia is thousands of miles away from England. But New York is just across the river.'

IN England you know for instance that the Labour Party is for the nationalisation of various industries and the Conservatives are against it. In America such ideological clashes hardly ever occur. A practical issue may be whether the U.S. should give a large loan to Britain or not. In Siloam Springs (Ala) the loyal Democratic leader, with an eye on the Jewish inhabitants, may take up an anti-British attitude because of Palestine. In the next village, however, the bank manager's daughter may have an English fiancé, a former R.A.F. pilot, who is personally very popular and the Democratic Party leader will be inclined to say: 'Let the poor boy have the dough'.

All this may seem very confusing but, in fact, it is quite simple. The difference between the two main American parties is very sharp and well defined; it is more marked than the difference between Communists and right wing Democrats in any European coalition government:

(a) one party is in, the other is out;
(b) one party wants to stay in and the other tries to get it out.

(After all, in nine cases out of ten, what is the real source of a minister's greatness? Not his political convictions, not his ideas, not his speeches, not his reforms and not his bills, but the simple fact that he *is* a minister. And the greatest contrast to being a minister is not being a minister.)

Beyond and above all political parties stand two layers of society who really rule the United States of America. First of all the women. There are no American 'Dubarrys'. It is not the old *cherchez la femme* story. It is *cherchez l'argent*. Women as a rule do not work and they are supposed to spend nine-tenths of all the money spent in the whole

The Tories are against it

country. This fact places immense social, economic and political power in their hands. American society is a matriarchal society. Useless males are not exterminated as they used to be by certain tribes in Formosa; they are only condemned to manufacture useless things (such as certain types of novels and magazines, nearly all the films, cosmetics, radio programmes etc). Men are condemned to wear golden ties and socks with silver circles on them. If the poor males succeed in making some money, women systematically establish charity clubs to spend it in the most ingenious ways. The majority of these clubs propagate the noblest ideas and support very good causes; some others are latecomers on the field of charity. It is due to the women that many an American university or college is transformed (as Charles and Mary Beard put it) into ' a small school attached to a vast stadium'.

There is one class which stands even higher than women: children. All things are permitted to children. They may beat one another black and blue in the park and nobody dares to interfere. You may see one little boy kneeling on another, hitting his head on the asphalt pavement as hard as he can and repeating. 'D'you give in?' He will go on doing it until the other yells: 'I give in,' then he gets up, and the affair is duly settled. You must not interfere because children are sacred. The second little boy, lying on the pavement, is sacred, too; still, you must not interfere. I saw a little girl of fourteen reading poetry to a traffic policeman on the corner of Broadway and 44th Street. The policeman was desperate but he had to listen attentively. At Christmas time a million dollars worth of toys are destroyed in the department stores by children who try them out, but this is included in the expenses. When the *Missouri* (the battleship on which the Japanese armistice treaty was signed) was shown to the public and visitors were allowed on board, American children did more damage to her in one day than the combined Japanese navy and air force had ever hoped to do.

THE Americans are decent and good-hearted people. In Hungary we used to define a truly generous person as one who would give you his last shirt if you needed it. This definition would not fit the American. But if you have no shirt he would lend you some money to buy one, provided

(*a*) you buy it from him and
(*b*) you are not a Communist.

(In many cases a Communist is defined as a man who has no shirt.)

Prosperity makes America the country of unlimited possibilities. As too many people want to read there and many people can afford to spend a quarter on printed matter of one sort or another, more illiterate people live on their pen in America than the total number of illiterates in other, less fortunate countries.

The Americans have their own arts. Jazz is their music, comic strips their most admired pictures, magazine stories their literature, Hollywood films their most popular entertainment, skyscrapers their architecture and their newest ball-point pens can write under water. America is immensely rich, her people are steadily growing in number and they are—as prosperous people always are—kind, good, fair, generous and keen-minded. They feel that they have inherited a world and they are eager to lead it to new destinies.

They trust themselves because they are confident that they can mass-produce many more orange squeezers, electric potato peelers and yellow socks with green circles on them, for the benefit of all humanity. We know, too,

*The position of the American in his own estimation. The curvature
of the earth's surfaces renders it impossible to observe this position
without some distortion of perspective. The possible margin of error
in the above diagram is about the width of the Atlantic Ocean*

that God could make America a wonderful country if he only had the money.

*　　　　*　　　　*

But can we trust them as leaders? . . . When I was a small boy we used to play football every Saturday afternoon in the field (it would be called the village green in England). Our centre forward was always the same little boy, let's call him Sammy. There was always a great deal of argument as to who should be in the team and what position one or another boy should occupy. But there was never any argument about the position of the centre-forward. It had to be Sammy. He was not a very good player; he could not use his left foot at all. But he wanted to play centre-forward and centre-forward he played.

The ball belonged to him.

WISDOM FOR OTHERS

Il est plus aisé d'être sage pour les autres que pour soi-même.

It is easier to be wise for others than for yourself.

LA ROCHEFOUCAULD

Also, the prudent man looketh well to his going
Proverbs xiv. 15

I. ON MONEY

SHORT ECONOMIC NOTES

THERE is a general shortage of pound sterling in this country. Our economists keep talking of a dollar shortage—indeed of a general shortage of foreign currency. Personally I have never been aware of being short of Dutch guilders or Swedish kronen. I have never been at a loss at my inability to pay out 175 drachmai or 3 escudos at short notice. But I never have enough pounds sterling. I have never received my own personal share of Marshall Aid. I know that it would not exceed seven or eight pounds in any case, but I do think it is most unfair to spend my money on ball-bearings when I have difficulty in paying my rent.

As a matter of fact I have more foreign money than I wish. The translation rights of my books were sold to a number of Continental publishers. My London publisher usually conducts lengthy conferences with foreign firms, achieves 8·50 per cent in royalties instead of 8·25 per cent as originally offered and conscientiously keeps me informed of the negotiations throughout. At last the contract is signed, whereupon we all congratulate each other and spend a lot of money on drinks and dinners in honour of our foreign friends. Later I receive news that my book has appeared and I make enquiries about my money. Then I am told that the National Bank of the country in question is almost as short of pounds sterling as I am. Consequently the money cannot be transferred. But I am not to worry. Should I wish to journey there (a return ticket costs only £80, to be paid here in British money), then the equivalent of £8 per day will be released. I may spend that money on anything I may dream of, excepting jewels, cameras, typewriters, any kind of industrial product, drinks, travel or food. I must guarantee to spend at least seventy-nine days in the country. I am warned, at the same time, that this is a serious infringement of the British currency regulations whereby I would make myself liable to seven years' penal servitude. There is no need for anxiety, however, as my books are selling fairly well.

I much prefer the arrangement made by a small East European country. They offered £50 outright for the—let us say—Cyrillian rights of my book. My publisher laughed derisively at this offer and asked for £200 advance and royalties. The Cyrillian gentleman brushed this offer aside with a supercilious smile and told him that the book would be published in any case, but should we refuse his offer, we would not get a penny. So my publisher signed the contract in a hurry, the Cyrillian gentleman took us out for a drink and supper and asked me to pay the bill. The book was duly published and the £50 never paid. I received a nice letter telling me not to worry: the book is selling very well.

The procedure adopted by another country gave me still less trouble. The copyright was stolen, the book printed and serialised and the only compensation left to me was the hope that it would prove a flop. But, at least this time, there was no correspondence, no negotiations, no drinks and dinners. I saved £5 net on the transaction. This was one of my best export deals.

The Greeks have a word for it

Nothing worries me as much as not having enough money. When I make a few pounds here and there, I add a little from my own savings and send it to the Chancellor of the Exchequer. It is a terrible feeling not to be able to feed your own Chancellor of the Exchequer. The knowledge that he may go about hungry or ill-clad, just because you are not able to support him, is humiliating and demoralising. On the other hand, nothing gives you more pride and satisfaction than the feeling that you have made a few more pounds for Chancie, so that he may be able to buy more ball-bearings, artificial manure and the other things he likes so much.

ON THE STANDARD OF LIVING

I DO not know how it is with other people, but my standard of living is unaffected, whether I earn much, little or nothing. I have always lived what may be termed a normally wretched middle-class life in whatever circumstances I found myself.

In Budapest twelve years ago, at the age of twenty-five, I had a large income as a journalist. I lived with my parents who were well off. My father accepted no contribution from me towards the household. I paid no rent, nothing for the telephone, electricity, laundry and many other items which make life so expensive. It is true that I ran a car but I had no expensive habits, did not drink, did not gamble and never saw a horse-race in my life. I was paid for going to the theatre and cinema and still I never had a penny. How I did it, I cannot tell. I always lived well, ate well and was able to invite friends whenever I wanted to, but my ready capital never exceeded the equivalent of 7s. 6d.

In London my income became variable. It moved in an irregular curve, often touching the depths but rarely reaching great heights. First of all I received my salary from my Budapest papers, then for a while I had nothing, later I was paid a miserable salary, then a fairly decent one, then a pittance: but throughout these vicissitudes my way of living never changed. I was never in debt, but could hardly ever afford a new suit; I took my own car to the Continent; I flew to New York, but was—and still am—absolutely unable to buy a standard-lamp for our sitting-room. Somehow I can always buy new fountain pens which write in red, green and purple or a new edition of the *Encyclopaedia Britannica* for myself, a Swiss watch for my wife or a tricycle for my little son, but have to conclude major financial transactions to enable myself to purchase a half-crown book of stamps. I am sure that most people are much wiser than I am. They buy houses and maintain large families on a half or a third of my income, have large savings and lose less hats than I do. How they do it is beyond me. My income suddenly dries up, yet six months later my bank balance is doubled. Meanwhile I have been aware of no change. I have neither less money nor more money. My standard of living has been neither better nor worse. I am one of the major economic puzzles of our age, and I wish a clever economist would solve me.

I am not, however, unique and as support for the suggestion that one's standard of living is absolutely independent of one's income, I offer the following story from my own experience:

I had often heard of a famous and very generous financier in Budapest who had been known to distribute five-pound tips to butlers and commissionaires for holding his coat and who was in the habit of buying country houses and motor cars for his lady friends just as we might buy a bunch of violets. Then he failed and lost all his money. One day my editor told me he was going to see Mr. K (the one-time financier) and asked me to accompany him. As I had been given to understand that the man was living a miserable existence in distress and penury, I was somewhat surprised when we stopped in front of a magnificent house in the most fashionable part of the city. The villa was exquisitely furnished and full of precious carpets and silver and gold. A wonderful *déjeuner* was served by a liveried footman. On the way back, I asked my editor whether he had been joking

Riches are relative

about Mr. K's penury. " Oh no," he replied and went on to tell me the sad story. " His villa has not been sold by his creditors because the auction would cost a lot of money and the price would just cover his unpaid taxes and the Treasury would have priority over private creditors. His carpets and art treasures? The same thing. And the footman? Oh, Mr. K owes him so much that he cannot afford to leave him." So poor Mr. K, in fact, lived his miserable and distressing life in his own beautiful mansion, among El Greco and Degas paintings and was looked after by two servants and a cook.

All things considered, I believe it is fair to deduce from my experiences the following general economic rules:

(1) If a rich man is ruined he is still rich. If you and I seem to have collected a fortune, we still remain poor.

(2) The real difference between the working classes and the majority of the middle class is not the fact that workers make more money. The real difference lies in the way in which they spend their respective incomes. Take just one example: the working classes spend more on bicycles and bicycle repairs than the rest of the population put together; on the other hand you will not find one single worker who has ever spent £2 10s at X Brothers to hire a top hat and morning coat for another worker's wedding.

(3) It is easy to have enough money for luxuries; it is almost impossible to have enough for necessities.

HOW TO BE A MISER

PEOPLE may be divided, according to their attitude towards money, into two classes: one wants to *have* money; the other wants to *spend* it. One wants security; the other pleasure. Of these two extremes—misers and spendthrifts—the misers are the more logical, because security may give you pleasure, but pleasure cannot give you security.

There are no pure types, of course, but we may safely generalise. To save money for your children's education and buy a life-insurance is right—indeed, it is your duty. Looking into the future is altogether very laudable, but I look into the near future only. As it is always necessary for me to think of next Saturday or the first of next month, I am rarely preoccupied with my well-being in forty years' time.

Some drawing-room psychologists assert that parsimonious people are altruistic while spendthrifts are selfish. But why should a person who saves every penny for his *own* old age be deemed less selfish than one who spends his money on others? Or even on himself? The latter may be less wise but he is certainly no more selfish.

I am not prepared to give up my enjoyment at an age when I *can* enjoy books, travels and society in order to save up everything for my old age. I am absolutely sure that I have actually reached my present age; I am not at all convinced that I shall be alive at the age of seventy-two or even forty. I have no desire to save up for my tomb. I have been badly dressed throughout my life and cared so little about it that I do not wish to wear an elegant sepulchral monument after my death. Forget me if you can; or else, remember *me* but not my monument.

No, I am not going to save up for a mausoleum. I am not going to pay rent after my death as well as all my life.

The art of saving is not a simple one. If I try to cut down my smoking and buy one hundred cigarettes less a week, I say to myself: "Now I have saved about one pound, so (a) I may buy a book, (b) go to the theatre with my wife, (c) buy a toy for my son." In such cases, I have the gratifying feeling that I too can save if I want to, and am satisfied that I am not a Bohemian (I hate Bohemians), but a decent and reliable member of society. Slowly, however, I have arrived at an economic truth which may seem self-evident but is not: it took me thirty-five years to see it and most people spend their lives without ever realising it. It is this: to spend £5 just because you have saved £1 is no real saving.

The miser is that exceptional person who really *has* the money he does not spend on one thing or another. He is the person who walks two miles to save three halfpennies, which he puts in a sock or in the bank, and when he dies leaves £123,000 to the N.S.P.C.S. (National Society for the Prevention of Cruelty to Sardines). The real miser, generally speaking, loves settling things after his death. He thinks of his old age with profound joy. It will be simply lovely. He will be slightly senile, will have the gout, will not be allowed to drink alcohol or eat anything but mashed potatoes and will be prohibited from saying "How do you do" to women. Those will be the days!

The only hitch is that I have never seen a miser who in old age did spend the money he saved in his youth. It is always the sardines who inherit it. (He is usually

Life begins at eighty

unmarried as he refuses to keep a strange man's daughter.)

If you want to become a miser, you must never forget a simple rule. A miser cannot have so much money that he is able to do without a single penny. I should like to illustrate this rule by a story, taken from the life of a great miser.

In Budapest, at the age of seventeen, I was present when a very rich gentleman, the owner of twenty-two huge properties, sold one of his houses. The final act of this sale was concluded in a lawyer's office where I worked and I officiated by running little errands, handing the pen to the various signatories and blotting the contract after a party had signed it. I watched as the equivalent of £50,000 was counted down to the old man. (Cheques are hardly ever used in Budapest.) There was a mountain of money lying on the table. He counted it four times and then opened a dirty old brief-case and produced the documents relating to the house: insurance certificates, tenants' contracts, etc., a thick pile of papers held together by a rubber band. After pondering for a few moments, he removed the rubber band and handed the documents to the purchaser's lawyer. The latter scrutinised the documents carefully and found everything in order, then turned to our client and asked him casually: "Would you mind giving me that rubber band, too?" The old gentleman hesitated, threw a glance at his 50,000 pounds' worth of cash and replied:

"The rubber band? Certainly. For threepence."

ON POVERTY

POVERTY was a brand-new and exciting experience
for me when I came to England. In Hungary, I had had
almost everything I wanted; in England I started to be
in want. I loved it and was proud of it. I boasted about
being in difficulties; I reminded my friends that I could
not afford to go to the cinema with them and proudly
refused invitations; I polished my trousers every morning so that they should shine even more brilliantly. One
of my friends became irritated by my boastful behaviour
and told me off:

"Can't you new-poor stop showing off?"

I meditated on this remark for a long time. Why did I
parade my poverty? Why was I so proud of it? I thought
of many answers—few people are at a loss to find a
theory if they need one—but I knew they were all false.
It was almost ten years before I discovered the true
reason. I was walking in New York, somewhere near
Third Avenue when a loquacious little man started a conversation with me. After a few minutes he shouted at me:

"I am a Jew."

"All right," I nodded. "Don't get excited."

"I am a Jew," he repeated still louder. "I am proud
of being a Jew."

"Why?" I asked him.

He looked at me in great surprise.

"What did you say?"

"I asked you why you are proud of being a Jew."

He hesitated for a few seconds:

"I've always been proud of being a Jew."

"I've got that," I said, "but why?"

We walked together in silence for half a minute. He
thought the problem over and finally declared:

"I guess it's like this. I am proud of being a Jew because if I were not proud I would still be a Jew."

So many of the poor are proud, too. This snobbish new-poor attitude was in the late forties greatly encouraged by the arrival of an unexpected newcomer to the ranks of the newly poor—Great Britain. She was almost as proud and boastful about being penniless as I used to be. Britain joyfully declared three times a week that she could not afford to buy petrol, machinery or meat; she announced with pleasure that she had to export all the goods she was manufacturing, and her people at home were only too pleased to starve; she was almost as proud of depriving her population of new clothes, new motor cars and a few slices of ham as some of the " popular democracies " were of announcing the manufacture of a new tractor or of utility shoes. Britain borrowed from her rich cousin but at the same time, with the eternal touchiness of the poor, spoke of self-respect and the necessity of standing on her own feet. A permanent problem of the poor is how to accept gifts of money with dignity. Britain has given a shining example to her fellow-poor and we are all proud of the distinguished company.

When I speak of poverty I do not mean penury and destitution. This is quite a different problem, a shameful state of things. Nor is my main worry the fact that Miss Betty Grable makes much more money with her legs than Professor Einstein with his head or that a great scientist never fetches such a good price as a great football player: it is that the not-too-talented son of a plumber will never have a ten horse-power car in his life.

Value for money

I am talking, in fact, of the poor like myself and most of us, who cannot afford to buy a lot of books, a radiogram, a television set, a film camera, a projector, to go for a cruise round the world or any other primitive necessity of life.

We have, however, certain justifications for our snobbish new-poor attitude:

(1) We are in a much more secure position than the rich. We may rest assured that whatever tragedies may befall us, we remain poor. We do not need to live in dread lest economic depressions, new inventions or state intervention may deprive us of our poverty.

(2) We are more honest than the rich. I used to argue that honesty has as little to do with one's financial situation as with one's religion or colour of hair. I was compelled to notice, however, that there are certain types of crime we never commit. None of our fellow-poor has ever spent two thousand pounds illegally abroad; none of us has ever cheated on his excess profit tax, or smuggled a mink coat through the customs for his wife, or lent large sums of money at excessive interest.

(3) We are much more modest. Only the rich are insatiable. No rich man considers himself rich enough; but I consider myself poor enough.

The great trouble is that we are no good as business men in our family. My younger brother is, it is true, a shade better than I am. Some years ago, he offered to buy my birthright for 2 pengös (about 2 shillings). I needed the money badly so we concluded the deal. I am not quite sure how he utilised his newly acquired right, but the whole story proves beyond doubt that he would know how to invest his money if he had any. Years later in New York, his little daughter Kitty, aged three, was bullying him to play cards with her. My brother first of all explained that playing cards was no pastime for little girls; upon this argument being rejected he said that he would not play with her as she had no money. This argument was also of no avail, so my brother suggested that Kitty should stake the pocket money, due to be paid her in later years. Fortune seems to have favoured my brother, and he won a considerable sum. They went on playing on many occasions thereafter, and the situation at present is that Kitty will get no pocket money until she reaches the age of twenty-one, and will then start paying her father $10 a week.

Personally I have made only one successful business deal in my life. I had a painting which I detested and wanted to get rid of it. When an American friend, a well-known collector of miniatures, visited me I offered him the picture for sale.

" But this is no miniature," he replied. " It is just a painting of ordinary size. Rather large, if you ask me."

" You seem to miss the point," I replied with a slightly ironical smile. " This is a miniature. In fact, this is the world's largest miniature."

" No kidding? " said the art collector, deeply impressed. The price he paid was considerable, but not unduly large for an artistic rarity.

" No kidding? "

II. ON SOUL

ON OTHER PEOPLE'S FAULTS

ONE would suppose that it is easier to bear small faults than great virtues. It is, I agree, hard to put up with a lady who refuses to stop being charitable; you may indeed feel inclined to kick a person, and kick him hard, who keeps giving you fatherly advice; it is not always easy to refrain from violence if someone keeps sacrificing himself for you. But there is another side to the picture. Imagine a man who is said to be admirably brave in great fires but has an unbearable giggle. However fair you intend to be, you must come to the conclusion that great fires, unfortunately, are only too rare, whereas he giggles much too often. Or imagine a lady who is kind to her aged mother but keeps talking about poultry-farming. (And let us suppose, just for sake of argument, that you are *not* her aged mother.) However big-hearted you may be, one day you are sure to make up your mind that you have learnt enough about poultry-farming and decide to avoid her for the next ten years.

The truth is that it is much easier to forgive great virtues than small faults.

And—I must add—it is easier to forgive great vices than small faults.

Suppose that a man has a slight inclination for fratricide. He may still be a good-mannered, witty and altogether agreeable person. And, after all, how many brothers does an average man have? But if someone makes a habit of telling you jokes and repeating music-hall stories, and does it every time you meet and all the time you are together. . . ? Or a man may be a Hollywood script-writer. This you may forgive—after all everybody has to live (I do not quite see why, but this maxim seems to be generally accepted). Should he have, however, the habit of leaning right into your mouth when talking, that is quite a different matter.

This is indeed the rule generally followed in our society. I never heard anyone say: "Don't invite So-and-so, he's always stealing hats," or: "Let's refuse his invitation because he is a bit slow in paying his income tax." But I often heard remarks like: "To hell with him, he is a brilliant man but never stops talking," or: "Yes, he may be the greatest mathematician in Lancashire, and I'll certainly go and consult him as soon as I come across a particularly odd spherical triangle, but he keeps scratching his bald head and I don't like that at all."

The main thing is to remember that there is no need to be patient with other people's faults. You are sure to find most irritating those faults which you possess yourself to a larger or smaller degree, so it would be very selfish of you to forgive them. Besides, why should some wretched fellow get away with your most repulsive habits?

"If you see what I mean——"

HOW TO BE THE CENTRE OF THE UNIVERSE

I HAVE little doubt that Galileo deserved his fate. Copernicus, Kepler and Tycho Brahe were only slightly better. It is very silly to say that the earth is not the centre of the Universe. It is. And you are—as you always thought—the centre of the earth, consequently of the Universe. The earth is many thousand million years old; man seems to be a million years of age and it was six hundred thousand years before he learnt how to speak. About six hundred thousand years elapsed between man's appearance on the earth and the end of the Stone Age. No matter—you are quite right in believing that (a) you are the centre of the Universe, (b) it *is* of immense importance whether you like shepherd's pie or not and (c) that God will be very angry if you play cricket on Sunday.

I know that modern science takes another view, but even modern science may be wrong. For instance, physics teaches you that the nearer you go to a seemingly small object, the larger it looks. Quite the reverse is the truth in the case of great men. The nearer you go to them, the smaller they seem. Philosophers went on arguing from the ancient Greeks through Descartes to Berkeley, whether we do or do not exist and whether material exists at all. I take no side in this learned argument although I have always paid my income tax on the assumption that the income-tax collector and my income existed. It is quite possible, however, that the world does not exist after all, in the objective sense; it exists, however, in the subjective sense. *Your* world exists and there can be no doubt that you are the centre of your own world. When you die, *that* world comes to an end.

Being the centre of the world, you had better make others realise this fact. Sometimes this is not easy, because people often believe that *they* are the centre of the world which—as I have just proved—is quite mistaken.

If you are a baby, your position is very good. You are the strongest person in your family; you have all the rights and no obligations. If they do not like washing nappies—well, they jolly well have to. You just howl as loud as you can and they—silly people—labour under the misconception that if they pay no attention to you, you will be quiet and go to sleep. Do not give in. Just carry on and they will pay you all the attention you want. I know. I am not only a father but used to be a baby myself. It depends on you, and on you alone, when they can eat, when they can go out and whether they can sleep at all. They love you and curse you; they swear at you and try to bribe you. But in the end they will obey you because you are the only absolute dictator in this world and your power starts fading only as you grow up.

When you grow up, you still like ordering others about just for the fun of it. Your position has become much weaker but do not give up. You may first of all try the direct approach—ordering people about and telling them what to do. They may obey; but they may not, and in that case the indirect approach is better.

Try nervous breakdowns. If your husband does not want to go to the theatre when you do—just have a nervous breakdown. Any doctor and most of your lady-friends will teach you how to have one. It is quite easy and worth the trouble. About three nervous breakdowns a year will bring any more or less decent man to his knees. Between attacks, fear of a new breakdown will operate satisfactorily. Your husband will possibly be not un-moved by the prospect of ruining your health and bring-ing you to an early grave by staying at home working, instead of taking you out to restaurants, by not increasing your dress allowance far beyond his capacity and by sundry other brutalities. If he is, it is too bad. In that case, try the martyr-attitude.

Suffer. Suffer conspicuously, loudly and with the ut-most propaganda. Does he want to stay in again and work till 4 a.m.? Oh, well. Of course, he must think of himself. You are not the type to complain. You may cry in secret, when only four or five people see you, but you do not complain. You wanted to go out to-night to see an American musical comedy. It is true that it has been on for eight years and is very unlikely to come off before we all die but, as it happened, you wanted to see it to-night. Still, your one little wish in life does not really matter. You are quite pleased to live the drab, dreary life of a suburban housewife. No, to-morrow will not do. But please do not give it another thought. You are prepared, nay, pleased to die of bore-dom in such a good cause.

For older people the " Of course, nobody listens to Auntie Sarah " attitude may be recommended with con-fidence. Nobody listens to Auntie Sarah. Nobody cares for Uncle Tom. You just listen to that boxing com-mentary on the wireless, all eleven of you, just because you are interested. Why care that Auntie Sarah wants to listen to "Family Favourites", which everybody else detests? Yes, you just go out to that lecture, why care that Uncle Tom wants to play chess? "I'll die, in any case within the next thirty or thirty-five years and then

The martyr's rôle

everybody will be happy to get rid of me (that is, everybody who will be still alive)."

You see the idea—strength through weakness. A simple bully will be defied. People will sooner or later revolt against him and feel like heroes. So develop some reliable weakness and you can call the tune for all the others. Who will fight the old, the young, the weak, the ill? And as far as you are concerned, you are not really a tyrant, you are not an unbearable nuisance who frustrates everybody. Oh no—you just give them a chance to be unselfish and noble, and to face up to facts. The fact that you are the centre of the Universe.

Years ago in Budapest I attended the funeral of a talented Hungarian actor, who died too young to become truly great. His director—a very able man and a poetic soul—delivered a funeral speech:

"*I* it was"—he said almost in tears—"who first noticed your great talent. *I* who took you out from the School of Dramatic Art and gave you your first stage contract. It was *I* in whose theatre you achieved your remarkable and promising successes. In *my* production of *King John* and *Cid* you established your fame, and ultimately it was on the stage of *my* theatre . . ."

At this moment the corpse sat up, looked at him with reproachful eyes and asked him very modestly:

"Excuse me, sir, but who is being buried here: you or I?"

HOW TO BE A NYMPH

The nymph is closely related to the class just described. You play the part of the semi-divine maiden of the sea, the mountains and the woods who knows nothing of this world. You do not know how to switch on the light so somebody else has to switch it on for you. You do not know how to look up a train in a time-table so somebody has to look it up for you. You do not know the town and have no idea where to change a bus or an underground train so someone has to accompany you wherever you choose to go. In your adorable ignorance you order a dozen oysters and a bottle of Madeira in a restaurant, because it just does not occur to you that liver sausage and an orange squash would be cheaper. You have no idea about such disgusting worldly things as money. Your friend just has to smile at you and say to himself: "How charming! How innocent!" And pay the bill.

It is very advisable to keep on using baby-talk. You chirp: "Little Adelaide (that's you) wants another double whisky." And add with an angelic smile: "Neat." Three gallant youths will rush to get it for you. Or you purr: "Little Adelaide would *love* that ruby ring, it would go so well with her nice blonde hair. Will Uncle Robert buy that teeny-weeny ruby ring for little Adelaide?" (Never mind if Uncle Robert is only twenty-two; it is not a matter of age; it is a matter of cash.)

If you are expecting some visitors, do not hesitate to ask your aunt to cook the supper or prepare the sweets: "You do it so much better. My friends still keep talking about that lovely roast duck (or sausages or Welsh rarebit) you made last time." You settle down to read *Vogue* and she will be delighted and proud to do it for you.

Cartier & Cie

Bob's your uncle

Useful phrases: "You are too wonderful for words. . . ." "I really do not know where I would be without you. . . ." "I love watching you doing things. . . ."

There exist some male nymphs, too. If you desire to become a male nymph it is better and more manly to choose the "you do it so much better" line, than to play the timid or ignorant. A good friend of mine had his garden dug up by a neighbour because he kept telling him what an inimitable digger he was. It is true that after two days' hard labour the neighbour wanted to stop, but my friend repeated to him most solemnly that nothing gave him more pleasure than to watch him dig (which was the honest truth), so he carried on for three more days and finished the job.

HOW TO DAZZLE

It is not enough for you to know you are the centre of the Universe. It is essential that other people, too, should feel your superiority. As it is not very easy to be good at your job and be satisfied with the notion that you are a decent person doing some good work according to your best abilities, you must use some helpful devices.

Do not forget that the world is small. In fact, it is as small as you make it. To be an influential person in world politics is a very high and almost unattainable aim for an ordinary mortal; to become the greatest painter in Great Britain is a tough proposition; to be revered and acclaimed by a nation or by half of the world is given to a Franklin Roosevelt or Winston Churchill, but few others. But you have a good chance of becoming quite an influential person in the Chipping Norton Debating Society; you may become the best painter in

Epping; and you may be revered and acclaimed by your family. So make Chipping Norton, the Epping Chess Club and your family your whole world. Really—what else matters when we come to think of it? The smaller you make your world, the greater your chances are. Your mother will always like your poetry—mine even liked my singing. Should you establish a one-man firm— the British Universal Button Factory Ltd.—you may shine in the eyes of your secretary as an important and truly great business man.

Sigh a lot, be always tired and say things like this: "I must do everything myself. . . ." ("Myself", by the way, is a wonderful word. How much more impressive it is to say: "I'll do it myself", than just: "I'll do it.") Or say: "This whole wretched machinery would stop if I did not look after everything myself." If you are a small firm, or a one-man firm, such a remark is about as meaningful as to say: "I don't know who would clean my teeth if I did not clean them myself." But most people will not notice it.

At a meeting of other business men you may be small and silent fry; the Board of Trade may turn down all your applications and call your activities unessential; your competitors and business associates may laugh at you. But retire to your own little office, sigh deeply, sink into a huge armchair, pick up a tremendous file of documents, speak on three telephones at the same time, dictate a letter to an earl—and the admiring glances of your secretary will compensate you for the lack of understanding in a selfish world.

If you need criticism—since criticism is very reassuring on some occasions—ask people who are dependent on

Small fry

you. They will tell you unhesitatingly, looking you in the eye (not just whispering behind your back), that all your ideas are epoch-making, that your failure is due to other people's wickedness, that your only great fault is excessive magnanimity and that you are altogether a brilliant and admirable fellow. Any man who wants to borrow a large sum of money from you, will tell you quite openly that he thinks you are very generous. Any painter who is keen on painting your portrait will declare firmly that yours is the most remarkable and interesting face since Julius Caesar.

There is always *something* in which you are superior to your neighbour. He may be a better bowler, but you may have the longer beard; he may have an uncle knighted but you may know how to say " Ladies " and " Gentleman " in Turkish; he may play the piano better but you may know Arthur Askey personally. You need to know, or do, or have really very little, to feel superior to your fellow-creatures. I have heard people vie with one another as to who has the larger feet, who knows the name of less foreign capitals or whose illness is more painful. In jail the habitual criminal under a sentence of seven years' penal servitude will look down (with the devastating contempt felt by professionals against amateurs) upon a man who is in just for a couple of months for a trifling black-market offence.

Shortages, generally speaking, used to do a great deal to heighten people's self-esteem and power. (The only power I am personally keen on is a little more purchasing power.) There were many shopkeepers who just tried to distribute fairly the few goods they had, but this was the wrong psychological approach. If you were a little tobacconist you could become a great worldly power in the eyes of a wretched fellow who implored you to give him ten Weights. If you decided to say " no ", you said it, as a rule, with gusto, with cruel pleasure and triumph. After all, can there be a nicer and more uplifting moment in a tobacconist's life than to refuse ten Weights to a man who is obviously dying for a cigarette? You said " no " imperiously and said it in such a way that he knew that you could have given him even ten Players if you had chosen to. Bless the shortages, they made you great, O greengrocer and flat agent, O publican and fish-monger. You had all human happiness under your counter and IT ALL DEPENDED ON YOU. There were some rare moments in life when even a lavatory attendant, regulating a docile but easy queue, seemed a man of power, importance and, above all, influence.

✧ ✧ ✧

This was the position in 1950 or so. Things have now changed to some extent. Yet, the truth remains that general misfortune makes more people happy than miserable.

THERE are some people who just cannot admit—or even see—that they may possibly be at fault. In England, however, most people have moral courage and they have learnt the formula: "I'm sorry, my fault." They insist upon it. You must not argue and say that it was your fault, because they get very angry. Once in North London I saw two cars collide and smash up each other's wings. Both drivers jumped out of their cars, shouting, "Sorry, it's my fault." Neither of them even looked at the smashed wings and broken lamps, but a sharp quarrel ensued as to whose fault it was, each claiming the absolute and exclusive responsibility for himself.

These magic words, "Sorry, my fault", are freely abused. The idea is this: what can people do to such a decent, straightforward, open-hearted chap who always declares that everything is his fault? He arrives at his office half an hour late. He does not tell tales about traffic jams and trains being late, even if one of these was in fact the sole reason for his delay. He says: "Sorry, it is my fault. I overslept."

Of course, it is manly, decent and right to take the blame if you have committed a mistake. But many people seem to think that it is even more manly and decent if you are as innocent as a newly born lamb. It shows that you are not only human—well, you commit mistakes—but also courageous and honest. Criticism is silenced. One cannot quarrel with a man who says it is his fault, insists upon this and proclaims it with pride.

I think religion is to a great extent to blame for this light-hearted mentality. Many types of Christian religion and the Jewish religion teach us that we may do as we like and get away with it provided that on certain days

" Sorry, my fault "

or occasions we duly and sincerely repent. I believe that a man can improve; but no one can improve retrospectively. You may be a more decent chap now than you were in the past; but you cannot be a more decent chap in the past than you really were. Nothing that was said can be unsaid; nothing that has been done can be undone. You may call your wife a silly cow on Tuesday and the only treasure in your lonely life on Wednesday. But you cannot explain to her on Wednesday that, when you called her a silly cow the day before you really meant to say that she was the only treasure in your lonely life. You may try, of course, but only eighty per cent of women will believe you.

In saying all this, I do not wish to hurt anybody's religious feelings. If I have, I am very sorry. My fault.

ABOUT ARGUMENTS

MANY people assert that good arguments and quarrels are the spice of life and particularly of happy married life. I must confess that I am rather bad at quarrels myself because, in most cases, I just couldn't care less. In my early youth my sister often complained against me, because she found me un-annoyable. My father, too, noticed that I followed, as a rule, the general tactics of the British Foreign Office, i.e. whenever he told me off severely for one thing or another, I fully agreed with him in principle, apologised if I had to, and went on doing things exactly as before. When he called me to account, reminding me that we had agreed on certain principles and asking why I had done the same thing again, I always had fairly convincing arguments ready to show that the same thing was not the same thing at all.

I have, however, studied the art of arguing and quarrelling and I may be able to offer some good advice.

(1) Beware of facts. If you are having a heated debate as to whether Betty's birthday party was in the last week of December or in the first week of January; or as to whether the author of *Cyrano de Bergerac* is Racine or Voltaire—do not consult diaries, encyclopaedias or Betty herself. Any of these steps would be unfair because (*a*) it would nip a very lively argument in the bud, and (*b*) it would deprive your opponent of all further reasonable reply.

(2) Refer to authorities instead. " You can take it from me, young man . . ." . " I have heard it personally from Wilfred Pickles or Aneurin Bevan . . ."

(3) Be personal and impute all sorts of motives to your opponent. If a man suggests that pawn-brokers firms should be nationalised and you do not approve of this proposition, point out that he has been cited as a co-respondent in a divorce case so he had better remain silent. Or say that this is only a mean device to save his own mother's fortune. Never mind if (a) he has no mother, (b) she has no fortune and (c) this is no way of saving anybody's fortune in any case. A little mud always sticks. It is a general rule of life that should you touch mud with your gloves, it is never the mud that becomes glovey; it is always the glove that becomes muddy.

The spice of life

SHEER silliness does not make one a bore. A great deal of hard work or innate ability is needed in addition. Nor is it enough just to go around telling long shootin', huntin' and fishin' stories (or whatever subject one may choose) or to keep talking about one's health. I should not go as far as to say that the gentleman who keeps entertaining his fellows with thrilling stories about his acid stomach or about the extremely odd and occasionally stupefying behaviour of his intestines does not deserve the name of bore. But a paragon of bores needs some other qualities as well.

If anyone wants to be an arch-bore, it is a *sine qua non* that he be a solemn and dignified person, taking himself deadly seriously. A light-hearted, foolish chatterbox may be irritating; but he is a feather-weight. I am concerned with heavy-weights.

The bore often wears a beard and/or monocle. I do not say that only bores wear beards and monocles but these insignia awaken suspicion. He always uses long words instead of short ones. Instead of saying " nice day " to the hall-porter, he will speak of " gratifying atmospheric conditions "; instead of giving sixpence to the waiter in a tea-shop, he will leave a " minor monetary gratuity ". This is the air he breathes and brings with him. When he comes into your flat, it becomes your family abode; your son becomes your male offspring, your wife your loyal spouse and you, yourself, instead of being just a chap he knows, become a *pater familias*. He is not just there to have a chat, he performs a valedictory address. When he is gone, at last, you do not think of him as a bloody bore, but as a sanguinary, fatiguing citizen. Everything is over life-size around him

Signs of ill omen

which makes him so artificial. Life, namely, is just life-size.

He has a sense of humour of some kind. He may meet you and say without a word of introduction: " Have you heard this one? " and rattle off a joke which, by the way, may be quite a good one. He can repeat a good story, but he will never make a tolerable, original remark. He speaks as if his part had been written for him by a mediocre dramatist; he acts as if he were carrying out some stage instructions with meticulous care. When he strokes your little son's blond head, he is fully aware that " now I am amiable with youngsters ". When he is courteous to a messenger boy, he does it with the air: " We must show tolerance and understanding to the lower classes." He knows his own place and keeps others in their right place. Whether he goes to a meeting or to the lavatory, he is always performing an onerous social duty. Even when he drinks a glass of gin and French, he is consciously jovial and chummy and enjoys social life, not because it is nice to have a drink sometimes with friends, but because he understands it is done. No man or woman is just an ordinary human being for him—like himself—everybody fits into some classification: a member of the weaker sex, his superior, his inferior, his senior, his junior, his better, his worse, a professional man or " the poor ".

He is virtuous and wears all his dazzling virtues in his buttonhole. He is dogmatic and everything has its proper place in his neat and orderly brain, just as each pair of his shoes has its regular and unchangeable place at the bottom of his cupboard. Things are either white or black; either good or bad. Crime is bad, virtue is good; cats are shrewd, dogs are faithful, priests noble, foreigners funny, sergeant majors vulgar, men of art refined. The world is such a simple place. He never uses phrases like: " yes, but . . ." or: " up to certain extent . . ." or: " although ".

You cannot find anything really stupid in his conversation; but you may have known him for five decades and you will not remember one single observation he has made on any subject under the sun. The real bore keeps explaining the obvious. He would explain for your benefit that everybody would be better off if wages and salaries were higher and prices lower; that the atomic bomb is a frightful weapon, much more terrible than the Roman catapult and, unless common sense prevails, our civilisation will come to an end; that if everybody would be thoroughly unselfish and think of others instead of himself, the world would be a better place.

The great bore is quite a good dish; all the ingredients are excellent, but he is prepared without salt and spices. Something is lacking in him, something that makes a dish a dish and a man a man. You just cannot swallow him. Spit him out.

III. ON MEN AND WOMEN

BEWARE OF LOVE

BY means of posters, advertisements, pamphlets, lectures and serious scientific books, people are taught how to avoid or cure 'flu, smallpox, a broken ankle and mumps; at the same time the major part of the world's literature (which is not to be confused with world literature), almost all the films, magazine stories and radio plays persuade you in an indirect way to catch a much more dangerous disease than any illness, universally known under the name of *love*—its scientific name being *dementia praecox temporalis*.

The main symptoms of the disease are these:

(1) The germ—a charming young lady in some cases, not so charming and not so young in others—makes the silliest and most commonplace remark and you consider her wittier than Oscar Wilde, deeper than Pascal and more original than Bernard Shaw.

(2) She calls you Pootsie, Bimby, Angelface, and other stupid and humiliating names; you are enchanted and coo with delight.

(3) She has no idea what is the difference between UNESCO and the L.C.C. and you find this disarmingly innocent.

(4) You expect her to behave like a cocotte of the *Folies Bergères* towards you and like a morbidly prim Victorian schoolgirl towards everybody else; and in some cases it takes you years to discover that the position is precisely the reverse.

(5) Whenever she flirts with others and is rude and cruel to you, you buy her a bunch of flowers and apologise to her. If she misbehaves seriously, you buy her jewellery.

The overwhelming majority of novels, short stories, films, etc., teach you that this dangerous mental and physical ailment is something glorious, desirable and romantic; who are you to question the wisdom of this teaching? You are expected to take the lesson of these high authorities to heart and believe that the world is mostly inhabited by lovers and murderers or a combination of the two: lovers who commit murder and murderers who fall in love.

Certain axioms underlie the teaching of this kind of literature:

(1) "Love is natural"—we are told—"animals also fall in love." I have always felt inclined to protest against this statement on behalf of the animals. I am no authority on animal psychology, but I am sure that no bear has ever bought a diamond ring for a lady-bear, just because she showed some inclination to share his cave.

(2) "Love is absolutely necessary because the human race must live on." This premise—that the human race must live on—is unproven, but let us take it for granted.

The least intelligible thing of all is the fact that love is constantly confused with marriage. Even if we accept the thesis that love is all right because it is a "natural thing" we should, I think, insist on it being kept out of marriage. You are expected to choose your future spouse when you are absolutely incapable of so doing. You have to choose her or him when you are in love, i.e. when you think silliness wisdom, affectation real charm, selfishness a good joke and a pretty face the most desirable of all human attributes. You would never send a deaf man to buy your gramophone records, a blind man to buy your paintings, and an illiterate to choose your books; but you are expected to choose the person whom you are going to hear more than your favourite record, see oftener than any of your pictures and whose remarks will be more familiar to you than the pages of your most treasured book—in a state of deafness, blindness and illiteracy. You may be fortunate: there are a great number of good records, pictures and books around and even the deaf, blind and the illiterate may make a lucky shot. You may discover that there is nothing much wrong in your choice, except that you bought a rousing march instead of a pastorale, an impressive battle scene instead of a still life and a copy of *War and Peace* instead of *The Ideal Husband*. Or else, in two years' time, you may realise that silk stockings and the films she likes—or the game of billiards he is so terribly fond of—are not the only things that excite you and that to be called "Pootsie" over the age of thirty-five is slightly inappropriate. You may wish your wife knew that Vladivostok is not an illness of which Napoleon died after the siege of Sebastopol. But then it is too late.

I suggest:

(1) Any propaganda inciting to love (in films, short

Wrong record?

stories, novels, paintings, etc.) should be made a criminal offence. The author of such a piece should be sent to a desert island with his beloved for five years.

(2) Any person falling in love should be sent to quarantine in a similar way.

(3) Love should be abolished altogether.

MARRIAGE is different. It is a good institution, but I must add that a lot depends on the person you are married to.

There is no such thing as a good wife or a good husband—there is only a good wife to Mr. A or a good husband to Mrs. B. A sadist and a masochist may make an ideal couple, although few people would envy their way of life. If an irritatingly credulous and gullible woman marries a pathological liar, they may live together happily to the end of their days—one telling lies, the other believing them. A man who cannot live without constant admiration should marry a "God, you are wonderful" type of woman. If he is unable to make up his mind, he is right in wedding a dictator. One dictator may prosper in a marriage: two are too many.

The way to matrimonial happiness is barred to no one. It is all a matter of choice. One should not look for perfection; one should look for the complementary half of a very imperfect other half.

If someone buys a refrigerator it never occurs to him that it is a bad refrigerator because he cannot play gramophone records on it; nor does he blame his hat for not being suitable for use as a flower-vase. But many people who are very fond of their stomach marry their cook—or *a* cook—and then blame her for being less radiantly intelligent and witty than Georges Sand. Or a man may be anxious to show off his wife's beauty and elegance, marry a mannequin and be surprised to discover in six months that she has no balanced views on the international situation. Another marries a girl only and exclusively because she is seventeen and is much surprised fifteen years later to find that she is not seven-teen any more. Or again if you marry a female book-worm who knows all about the gold standard, Praxiteles, and Kepler's laws of planetary motions, you must not blame her for being somewhat less beautiful and temperamental than Marilyn Monroe. And if ladies marry a title or a bank account, they must not blame their husbands for not being romantic heroes of the Errol Flynn type.

You should know what you are buying. And as long as you do not play records on your refrigerator and do not put bunches of chrysanthemums into your hat, you have a reasonable chance of so-called happiness.

There are, however, some ways of wrecking your marriage even if you are perfectly suited to your spouse.

(1) The honeymoon mentality. Some people believe that marriage is a perpetual honeymoon. Not only do they believe that married couples spend their lives among the moonlit ruins of a medieval castle, holding hands, exchanging tender remarks and listening to the peaceful murmur of the sea, but—what is much more terrible—they would like to do the same. The main responsibility for this idiotic conception lies with the film studios. Ninety-nine per cent of all films end with the hero and the heroine getting married and this is called the happy ending, instead of the hard beginning. Most film-goers do not follow up the consequences. The marriage of the hero and the heroine means that instead of flirting in woods, kissing on the sands, pursuing gangsters, shooting spies and doing other

The application of Kepler's Law

thoroughly uninteresting things, they will at last settle down to a decent and thrilling life. They will do the washing-up together, clean their flat, cook Irish stew, meet all sorts of people, spend and save money and—if they are lucky—wash nappies. How dull are the moonlit ruins compared with a good book two people enjoy reading together. How dull is a spy-ring compared with a newly born baby.

(2) The second sure way of ruining a promising marriage is the magnifying glass. Look at everything through a magnifying glass. If your wife buys a new hat, call her a spendthrift; if your husband comes home half an hour late either from his office or from the pub, call him an inconsiderate pub-crawler who does not care a tinker's cuss for his beloved wife. If he wants to use the bathroom when you do, make a scene, quarrel, weep, shriek and have hysterical fits.

When I was young my father used to be very strict about food. My sister, my brother and I had to eat everything that was served up with the exception that each of us was entitled to reject one kind of food. I refused rabbit, my sister refused spinach and my brother rice pudding. This spinach rule (let us call it that) is very sensible. It is easy—or at least not terribly difficult—to comply with reasonable wishes. But in marriage we have to make some allowance for unreasonable wishes, too. If your husband likes sitting in a cold room with the window open, do not explain to him two hundred times that a cold room is cold and the open window makes it still colder. He is almost certainly aware of this.

Think of the spinach rule, let him freeze, and insist, for your part, on being allowed to spend every other afternoon snail-watching. He must refrain from shouting at you while you are watching your snails; in return he may open all the windows and enjoy the howling wind in his shirt-sleeves. The spinach rule is the secret of a happy married life as well as of smooth contact with all our lunatic friends, mulish bosses and whimsical employees.

(3) Be misunderstood. I personally never quite understood what it means to be misunderstood. I could never misunderstand anybody because I just did not know how to do it. There are some jealous persons who are always jealous, with or without reason; some worrying souls who are always worried if for no other reason than because there is nothing to worry about; similarly, there are some misunderstood women who are misunderstood as some others are red-haired or cross-eyed. "My husband does not see the poet in me." "My husband is always busy in the office, making a wretched £6,000 a year and never thinks of buying me a bunch of violets." It is no use trying to improve. You are irredeemably that brute who keeps her in luxury, gives her a thousand-pound clothing allowance, but never buys her a bunch of violets. It is no use buying a bunch of violets for her because (a) now it is too late, (b) you obviously think that everything can be put right with a wretched little bunch of violets. Remain the brute and let her suffer. And let her be misunderstood. If you have married one of these crossword puzzles, do not try to solve her. It is hopeless,

"The poet's fire that burns within"

because she keeps changing her clues. As a rule, she is even more complicated horizontally than vertically.

It is always easy for a mistress: she is a specialist. A wife has to be a wife, a mother, a cook, a nurse, a mistress, a housekeeper, a book-keeper and a society lady. Sometimes she is hopeless in all her tasks and you do not understand why. In such cases ask yourself: how did she become your wife? Ask yourself why you consented when she proposed to you. On the other hand, however excellent she may be in all these fields and however wonderful you are, it is never easy to live together with another person because even the kindest man may snore and the sweetest woman may love to listen to Music Hall on the radio. But one thing is certain: if every person were to use the same common sense and patience in his efforts to make his marriage a success as he uses to fill out a football-pool coupon, his expenses would be much less and his chances of success much higher.

ON DIVORCE

ONCE when I was about twelve, I read a story in a boys' paper about a big dance to which people were invited by huge posters with the announcement: " No entrance fee." Many went, danced and enjoyed themselves and then on leaving they were stopped at the door and requested to pay. " What do you mean? " they protested, " we were told that there was no entrance fee." " That's quite true," was the answer. " There was no entrance fee but there is an exit fee."

I considered that story at the time silly and impossible. Silly, indeed it was; but impossible? Look at the marriage laws of modern and civilised countries and especially the Anglo-Saxon world. There is no entrance fee; but there is a terrific exit fee.

Every contract, even a solemn alliance between nations, may be terminated by *either* party if due notice is given. Marriage may not be terminated even if *both* parties declare that they have had about as much of each other as they can possibly stand. The official explanation is that marriage is not an ordinary contract. If a silly girl of twenty-three and a hot-headed, scatterbrained, unemployed boy of twenty-one rush to the registrar, obtain a licence and get married in a few days' time, that is a sacred union, the foundation of our society.

Bad marriages may be the foundation stones of our society but they should not be. And it is only the bad marriages which are declared to be indissoluble as, obviously, no one wants to dissolve an ideal marriage. Is it the sacred foundation of our society to compel people to go on quarrelling for a lifetime? To compel two people who cannot stand the sight of each other to stay together—or at least to stop them from a second marriage, which Dr. Johnson (I think) called the triumph of hope over experience? Is it the sacred foundation of our society to increase unhappiness, bitterness and frustration? I dare say it is. Our society looks very much like it.

It is lucky that few people judge the English by their divorce laws. They would regard them as an immoral, undignified and ridiculously inefficient people, which they are not.

The English divorce laws seem to be the creation of a people excessively preoccupied with sex, which the English—once again—are not. Practically the only reason for divorce in Britain is adultery, as though the sexual relationship between the partners were the only problem that matters.

The English laws in many cases *compel* people to commit adultery. This being the only practical reason for divorce, poor, moral, mid-Victorian, prudish males have to associate with prostitutes in the hope that they will thus be able to get rid of perfectly decent women who don't happen to be the right persons for them. One may say that people should be more prudent *before* choosing a wife. One may, indeed, and quite rightly so. But one may also say that if people were more prudent, wise and sober in all their affairs, the world would be a different place and its people would be different people. I fully agree that our divorce laws may be absolutely perfect in a different world and for different people.

I have a great admiration for British judges. But it is painful for me to see one of His Majesty's judges sitting in a solemn court, listening day in and day out to all the details of how, how often and why Mrs. X committed adultery. Adultery, I have noticed, is more often than not committed in private. The legendary hotel maids and charwomen see two people in bed only when they want to be seen. A great deal of the evidence is prefabricated and quite a number of undefended cases are collusive. I know it, you know it, the parties know it, solicitors know it, counsels know it, the judge knows it, but we all pretend to believe every word of the tale. Such divorce laws are guilty of contempt of court because they do bring the courts into contempt. Many cases are farcical. I have nothing against a good farce, but these farces are cruel, because giving evidence in a divorce suit is torture. These farces are only unintentionally funny. Yes, I do love a good farce but prefer Mr. Danny Kaye in the leading part to a dignified, wigged and robed judge of the King's Bench Division.

The English are quite savage about their divorce laws. No government dare touch them radically, because they are afraid of losing votes and particularly afraid of the churches and old maids, who all believe that they, between themselves, have a monopoly of virtue. If the time has come to nationalise the mines and the railways, it is also time to secularise virtue.

The English divorce laws are puritanic. Macaulay said of the Puritans that they objected to bear-dancing, not because it caused pain to the bear, but because it gave pleasure to the spectators. Similarly, the divorce laws of those sex-starved Victorian prudes forbid divorce, not because it would cause pain to society but because it would give pleasure to the parties.

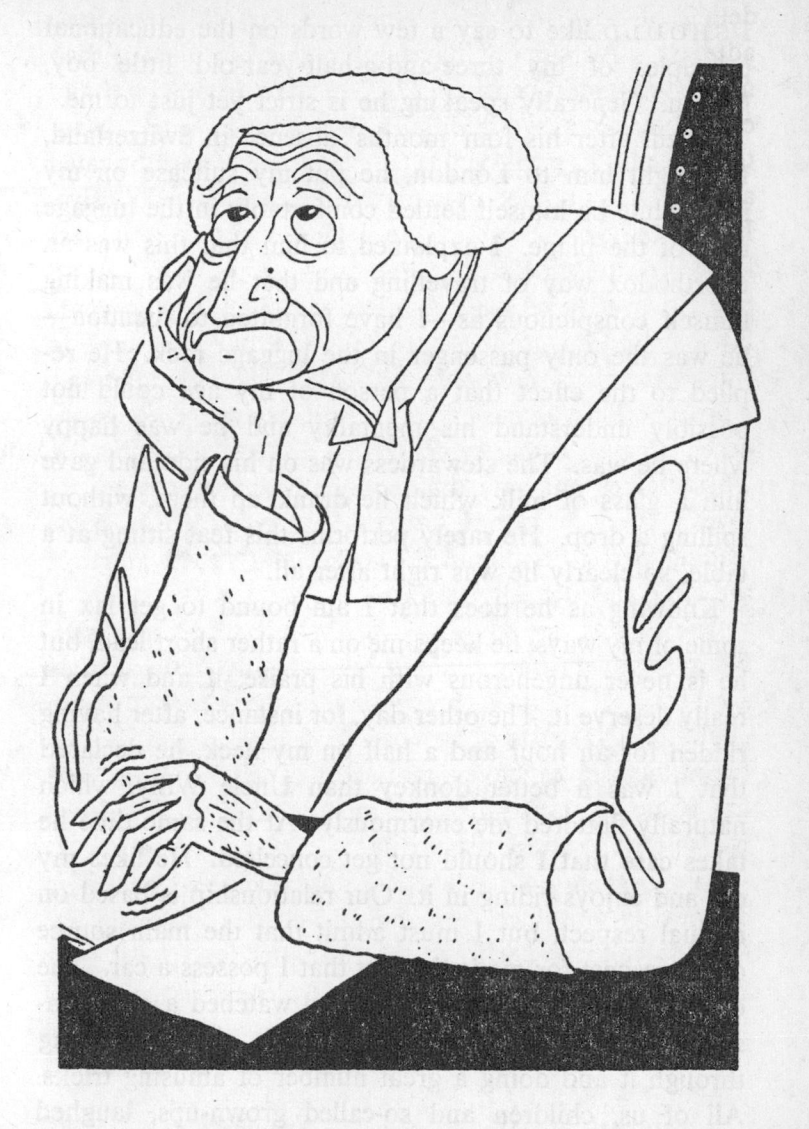

Tell me the old, old story

ON THE EDUCATION OF PARENTS

I SHOULD like to say a few words on the educational principles of my three-and-a-half-year-old little boy, Martin. Generally speaking he is strict yet just to me.

When, after his four months' absence in Switzerland, I brought him to London, he put my suitcase on my head while he himself settled comfortably in the luggage rack of the plane. I explained to him that this was an unorthodox way of travelling and that he was making himself conspicuous as—I have forgotten to mention—he was the only passenger in the luggage rack. He replied to the effect that a person of my age could not possibly understand his mentality and he was happy where he was. The stewardess was on his side and gave him a glass of milk which he drank up there, without spilling a drop. He rarely performs this feat sitting at a table, so clearly he was right after all.

Knowing as he does that I am bound to get lax in some of my ways, he keeps me on a rather short lead, but he is never ungenerous with his praise, if and when I really deserve it. The other day, for instance, after having ridden for an hour and a half on my neck, he declared that I was a better donkey than Uncle Willy, which naturally flattered me enormously. At the same time he takes care that I should not get conceited. He likes my car and enjoys riding in it. Our relationship is based on mutual respect, but I must admit that the main source of his respect for me is the fact that I possess a car. The other day we went to the Zoo and watched a chimpanzee playing with a tyre, throwing it about, jumping through it and doing a great number of amusing tricks. All of us, children and so-called grown-ups, laughed loudly, but Martin's face suddenly grew serious.

Playtime

"Daddy," he said, "that is a tyre."

"Yes," I nodded, not suspecting any danger. "That is a tyre."

"A car tyre," he said, half asking, half explaining.

"Yes," I agreed, "a car tyre."

He reflected for a second, then turned to me and declared softly but firmly, rather in the tone of a K.C. who has just carried out a successful cross-examination and has come to a conclusive point:

"Then the monkey has a car as well."

It was no use arguing. I thought I was lost. Luckily, however, the monkey stands quite high in his estimation so my chances are not spoilt altogether.

While trying to shape my character to his best advantage, he never stoops to rough methods. He employs reason and argument whenever possible. One day I tried to convince him that in taking one of his slippers off and placing it in the vegetable soup, he had acted wrongly. He took the slipper out of the soup and put it in again and explained:

"There's lots of soup like this."

Now we all know that chefs in London put all sorts of things in the vegetable soup, just in order to have "lots of soup like that". Judging by the result, and seeing to what extent it did fill his plate, I believe that a slipper is more effective and, I am sure, quite as tasty as anything I have seen in soups up to now.

Martin is spending only a few weeks with me in London before going back to Switzerland. The educational effects of his presence are manifold and beneficial to me:

(1) *No more laziness.* There is no question any more of lounging about in bed, getting up late and spending a considerable and precious part of the day doing nothing. Whatever time I may have gone to sleep, at 7.30 a.m. I hear a faint and polite voice calling "Daddy". By 7.45 a.m. the voice becomes a shade more impatient and by 8 it is definitely commanding and irresistible—and my day begins at eight o'clock sharp, Sundays included. I have led a healthy and sporting life since Martin has been here: I spend more time in the park than any of the keepers, do more running than the most diligent athlete, and—as the lift is Martin's favourite means of communication—the liftboy in our block has taken a few weeks' holiday because Martin and I do his job. As Martin takes it as a personal offence if anybody who gets into the lift dares to leave it, all the tenants in our block spend more than their fair share of time in the lift.

(2) *He cultivates the true British spirit in me.* Martin is a British subject by birth. Consequently he seems to be a paragon of true British virtues, the spirit of compromise ranking high among them. Due to my unfortunate Continental upbringing, I am still inclined to call a piece of white paper a piece of white paper and not "light" or "whitish" or "not so dark". This is deplorable—I am fully aware—but the force of habit is too strong.

The other day we had tea together—tea being the name of a meal consumed at 4.30 p.m. He was having milk and I coffee.

"Daddy is having tea," he declared suddenly. It

is one of his habits to make a running commentary on life.

"No," I replied, "Daddy is having coffee."

He shook his head and repeated:

"Tea."

"No, Martin," I argued with that unbearable obstinacy which is so characteristic of me, "sometimes Daddy has tea but now Daddy is having coffee."

He looked at me sadly as though he realised that it was unfortunate not to be the son of a native, but as it had fallen to his lot, he had to bear it with patience and fortitude. He half shut his right eye in an impish manner and suggested in a compromising voice:

"Tea-coffee?"

I knew this was the voice in which Chamberlain offered half of Czechoslovakia to Hitler.

"Tea-coffee," I nodded.

It was my Munich.

(3) *He gives me self-confidence.* This is one of the best educational effects he has on me. If I had any doubts about myself as a humorist, he has dispelled them completely. I put a pillow on my head as though it were a hat and he laughs aloud; I hide behind the cupboard and call out "Coo-coo" and he shrieks with joy. I am confident that, whatever the general opinion of people about my entertaining value, there *is* a certain age-group to which I do appeal.

(4) *I have now a broader and wiser view of life in general.* He has a wooden motor car of tremendous dimensions which he once propelled

Funny man

towards me with great force; as I was sitting on the floor, it came into very violent contact with my knee. "Ouch," I shouted. He stood up, walked to me and stated in the voice of a sage: "It doesn't matter." The philosophical implication of this remark was that people, generally speaking, make too much fuss of little things; worry too much about trifles and have quite unnecessary worries and excitements throughout their lives. He hit my knee—and what of it? He was right. In two minutes I forgot all about it.

This is real wisdom and betrays a truly happy disposition. This was not an exceptional case: next day I fell off a swing and later rolled down a flight of stairs and—I am pleased to report—he was not worried in the least.

(5) *He opposes mystification.* Whenever we play hide-and-seek, he hides himself with the greatest care, but when I come into the room saying, "Where is Martin?" he comes forward, declaring "Here!" and retires to his hiding-place again. Some of my friends and relatives maintain that the reason for this behaviour is that Martin is silly. This is quite wrong. His behaviour has some metaphysical implication: he is fully aware that we are pretending in any case, and as he is not the person to spoil anybody's fun, if it is a pleasure to me to play such silly games, he is prepared to bear with me. But he quite rightly reminds me that it is just a game and I must not take it seriously. Knowing how absent-minded I am, he wants to save me from hiding, and not being able to find myself for a few days.

Were he to stay here a little longer, he might have some hopes of making me quite a decent and useful member of society. The time being too short, his task is hopeless.

He is not quite dissatisfied, though. He summed me up with these words: "You are not a bad boy, Daddy, but a bit naughty." A board of directors after a two and a half hour's interview came to exactly the same conclusion, but expressed it much more pompously and used longer words.

EQUAL RIGHTS FOR MEN!

I THINK it is high time for the male population of the world to unite and organise. We want equal rights for men—and are prepared to fight for them.

I am ready to grant all political, social and economic rights to women, equal pay for equal work and everything they want. I want to see female judges, generals and priests. I go still further. I acknowledge that they are entitled to be—to use a well-known phrase—more equal than others, because, I venture to prophesy, it will always be the women who bear the children.

Between the two wars, the French Parliament once debated the problem of women's franchise. One of the representatives exclaimed in the course of an impassioned peroration: "You must give them the right to vote! Why to men and not to women? What is the difference?" The whole Chamber echoed the answer, like one man: *"Vive la différence!"*

Indeed, *vive la différence,* but:

(1) If women work as they should and they do, then they should not expect men to pay their bus-fares, taxis, dinners, etc. Leaving other considerations apart for the moment, I am quite prepared to take a young lady out to dinner and the theatre and take her home in a taxi. But then I should expect her to take me out next time, pay for my dinner and theatre ticket, and take me home in a taxi. Kissing hands is a silly Continental habit which they may overlook. I have tried to convert many ladies to my ideas, but they never seemed to see my point. So far, I have done all the paying. They protested that such things are not done and they did not want to

humiliate me. To which I would reply that I was not in the least touchy and urge them to pay. Whereupon they smiled at my ready wit, and ordered another brandy at my expense.

Why is this? Because laws are man-made laws, laws of a bygone, chivalrous, pre-cinema and pre-typewriter age and men are visited now for their selfishness and stupidity. They have lost their rights and kept their obligations. After 5.30 p.m. the chief accountant of a City firm still insists that he is a rococo courtier, and in the junior female filing clerk he is still determined to see a lady-in-waiting in the court of Louis XV.

(2) It is another anomaly that women expect men to give up their seats in buses, tubes and trains. Man, however, has solved this problem in a truly manly fashion. They do not give up their seats. At least not to old ladies, obviously tired ladies or badly dressed ladies. But should a pretty girl of seventeen come in, a whole row of rococo knights will jump up and perform all the gestures of a French quadrille in the best Versailles style.

(3) Why can we not sue women for breach of promise of marriage? Because we are not their equals. We cannot go to court, stating that the lady promised to marry us and we spent £2 10s. on a wedding ring, that we had some new shirts and pants made as part of our trousseau, that we had our flat cleaned by a charwoman for 7s. 6d., bought an extra bath towel and counted on getting a director's job in her father's plastic powder-compact manufacturing firm.

The age of chivalry

(4) How obviously underrated we are by the law is shown by the fact that damages are hardly ever paid for the loss of a husband. Any woman must feel terribly proud listening to a judge assessing her value in cash. She was a good housekeeper, £100; she was rather a good hostess, £50; but she was fond of telling stale jokes—deduct £30; her hair was dyed, deduct another £18; she cooked excellent Yorkshire pudding, add £33; but always over-salted the cabbage, deduct £5 10s. That makes it £129 10s. plus 33⅓ per cent purchase tax plus another £100 for repairs, so the final sum is £272 13s. 4d. Her bosom must swell as she learns that she is almost as valuable as a good horse or a pre-war Morris Ten.

What about me? If someone very wickedly enticed me away from my wife, why could she not say in court to the other woman: "He was a good cook, £50; he made paprika chicken better than anyone else I know, £5; he was terribly untidy, deduct £15; he always made a mess in his room with his cigarette ash, deduct £15; he made silly jokes about my most solemn ideas, deduct £15; he had the most terrible voice and no ear at all but kept singing Hungarian folk-songs and Gilbert and Sullivan duets all day long, deduct £15. Here you are, take this fiver and you may keep him."

It can never happen. Why? Because we are not equal with women.

I have a good mind to chain myself one morning to the railings of 10 Downing Street.

IV. A FEW WORDS ON THE WORLD

THE UTILITY MAN

I AM not a lofty character and this fact worries me a great deal.

I should love to be respectable, revered by my innumerable children and grandchildren, sit in a huge armchair, fulminate against sin, go to the church every Sunday morning, have at least two industrial knights among my friends, love cats a little more, have a jovial laugh and instead of suffering from a vulgar, slightly acid stomach, have the elegant and feudal gout.

I have not given up hope altogether, but I am in a bad way.

What is the world like to-day?

The Common Man is being slowly but surely replaced by a hyper-modern variation, the Utility Man.

I can still remember the times when human beings used to multiply by a certain biological process; to-day most of them seem to be manufactured on the assembly line. The production of this new Utility Man is cheaper and the result is more beneficial from various points of view.

The Utility Man does not need to think, which is a great comfort. In the old times you *wrote* your opinion to the newspapers; to-day you *read* your opinion in the newspaper. The ordinary citizen picks up his views from the daily papers, but we, really intelligent and independent people—you and I—wait for the weeklies. The problem of illiteracy has been completely solved: a great number of people do not know how to read (even when they happen to know the alphabet), but any child of three knows how to push the button of the television.

We wear utility clothes, live amid utility furniture in our utility houses, eat a utility diet, utter certain utility sentences (which we call conversation), read utility novels, see utility films, laugh at utility jokes. We start our days with the utility remark: " Lovely day, isn't it? " and finish it by switching off the utility lamp over our utility bed and kissing good night our utility wife or husband. We have been taught a great deal about the uniqueness of Man. Indeed, there are no two people in the world exactly alike. Nor are there two rolls exactly alike. On the whole, 98 per cent of people are about as unique as a Lyons roll. Townsmen and countrymen differ from one another about as much as the Oxford Street Woolworths differs from the Bishop Auckland Woolworths.

The appearance of the Utility Man may solve one of the outstanding problems of our age: the problem of individual rights. In ancient times there were individuals but they had no rights; to-day we have rights but there are no individuals. (In some parts of the world a degree of perfection has been reached: there are neither individuals nor rights—so the problem just does not seem to exist.)

Ancient kings used to rule by the Grace of God. Modern democratic governments rule by the grace of the radio and television. Every ancient revolution started by expropriating the gods; every modern revolution starts with an attempt at seizing the radio station. Give me the radio stations and a hundred able propagandists and

By grace of God

in two months I shall (*a*) turn Switzerland Communist;
(*b*) persuade all the inhabitants of Honduras to dye their
hair red and persecute those who refuse to do so and
(*c*) persuade the Kirgiz republic of the U.S.S.R. to ask
for permission to join the U.S. as its forty-ninth member
state. (To persuade the United States to accept them
would take a little longer and cost more.)

Our society is a free society.

In a free society you are allowed to say what you think.
But you are not allowed to think.

THE BIG TWO AND A HALF

TO-DAY three important ideologies face each other in the world. The American Way of Life, Communism, and the Third Force.

(1) The gist of the American Way of Life is that it is strictly American. It is not an export-article, otherwise Britain would have started exporting it long ago. Western Europe tries to build its existence—or at least its prosperity—on the fact that Americans have hard currency and soft hearts.

(2) The gist of Communism (as Krushchevism is called, just like Stalinism used to be) is that it has nothing to do with Communism. It is not revolutionary, it is not progressive and it is not international. To-day the Russians want to convert the British to Communism and the Americans want to convert the Russians to monopol-capitalism. This is obviously useless. If we could convert Russia to Communism, America to monopol-capitalism and the British Trade Unions to Socialism, this world would become a much better place, or at least, one easier to understand. No, Krushchev is not a Communist; he is not even a fellow-traveller.

(3) The Third Force is rather like the Third Programme: poor but respectable; highbrow and not very popular.

The real weakness of the Third Force (and the Third Programme at that) is that they are too good for a mediocre world. We live in a world of slogans and cheerleaders and the slogans of the Third Force inspire little enthusiasm at the moment. The misleading cries of the

Communists and the vociferous cheer-leaders of the Western Hemisphere may inspire you to fight and before you have time to examine the real content of their battle-cries and the true value of their ideas—you are dead. So this is all right. But we have failed to popularise our own slogans: " Long live Austerity! " " Long live the National Savings Campaign! " " Give us more subsidised sausages! " " Long live our free spectacles! " I personally would much sooner shed my blood for subsidised sausages and free spectacles than for the Eastern revolutionaries who are more afraid of world revolution than the most Blimpish Western shareholders. I am convinced that the British with their talent for muddling through, the French with their crystal-clear brains and dirty lavatories, and the smaller Western nations with their ancient traditions and a fair amount of Teutonic *Tüchtigkeit* represent the real genius of the human race. But we labour under a disadvantage, because " Proletariat of the World Unite! " is admittedly a more inspiring slogan than " Export more marmalade! " If the proletariat of the world do unite, they will be kicked in the pants by Russia; if we, on the other hand, do export more marmalade we—and they too— will live a fuller and freer life. We must popularise our battle-cries. It is really a matter of repetition and strength of voice: " Long Live Subsidised Sausages! " " Long Live our Free Spectacles! " " Marmalade-Exporters of the World, Unite! "

Many people believe in the Party Which Is Always Right. They believe that Russia is the country of the Revolution and that Krushchev is a Communist. Nothing

" Export or BUST! "

shakes their belief, not even the famous last words of a
Czech worker who, before throwing himself into the
River Moldau, not being able to maintain his wife and
three children, had scrawled on a piece of paper: "I
understand that the factory now belongs to me; but I
shall never understand why I kicked myself out."

ON JUDGING PEOPLE

T H E worst possible insult to any person is to tell him that he has no sense of humour; the second worst is to declare that he is not a shrewd judge of human nature.

Judging people, however, has become immensely difficult since Professor Freud wrought havoc with our knowledge of psychology.

I also have discovered a psychological law which is, I dare say, of considerable importance, but labours under three disadvantages:

(1) It has no Greek or Latin name of over ten syllables. It is simply called the Law of Duality and, unfortunately, this name may be quite clear at first hearing not only to any child but also to any psychologist.

(2) It has nothing to do with erotism, auto-erotism, narcissism, nymphomania, libido, or in fact anything really thrilling.

(3) I do not think it is true.

The Law of Duality is this. We cannot become perfect beings because our bad qualities follow logically from our best qualities and vice versa. For instance, if you always tell the harsh truth, you are bound to be rude; if you are, on the other hand, always kind and polite to everyone, you are very often bound to be untruthful. If you are a man of principles, you are bound to be stubborn; if you have a very flexible mind you are bound to have flexible principles. Even if you steal toys for your little son, you are likely to be—whatever else you may be in addition—a loving father.

The frontier between good and bad is often hardly discernible. Where is the sharply defined line of demarcation between a trusting nature and a credulous fool? Or between prudent caution and moral cowardice? The probability is that the same person is a lovable and trusting soul in one case and a credulous fool in another; he is prudent and cautious on Monday and a coward on Tuesday.

We must not judge any single characteristic in itself. Human characteristics have a chemical effect on one another, they become dissolved, mixed, blended and combined in a peculiar way and there are no psychological formulae to predict the result with certainty. Vanity, curiosity, a little sadism and inherent soberness may produce a great surgeon; the same ingredients without the inherent soberness may produce a sexual criminal.

Now I wish to summarise briefly three points which do *not* follow from this:

(1) It does not follow that every bad trait has its good side which equalises its effects. You would not say of a poisoned apple that it is all right, as it contains an equal amount of arsenic and vitamin.

(2) It does not follow that you should consider motives. You cannot afford to. Let us suppose that a little girl falls into the Thames and Smith throws himself into the water, drags her out and saves her life at the risk of his own, while Jones stands by placidly pretending not to have seen anything. A really great psychologist may explain that Smith is a braggadocio and an adventurer, only concerned to show off while Jones is the incarnation of modesty

whose only wish is to avoid personal publicity. Be a primitive soul, like myself, and call Smith a brave man and Jones a coward.

(3) It does not follow that if someone is kind and helpful to you, you should say: he must be a weakling and I despise the wretch. Nor does it follow that if someone kicks you, you should admire his manly strength and kiss his boots.

But it does follow, that we must treasure our vices and be cautious with our good characteristics because one could not exist without the other. It does follow that judging yourself or others you must not think of separable mental ingredients, but of the mixture only.

Beware of kindness—or rather do not trust it implicitly because in a bad mixture it may only cover a weakling and a liar.

Beware of too much sincerity and open heartedness; chatterboxes seem often very sincere.

Beware of promises; they are often given to please you to-day and not to be kept to-morrow.

Beware of fanatics; they are usually frustrated fools who do not even believe in their own doctrines.

Beware of too much chastity; because it is often practised and preached by people who would have liked to sin but could not.

Do not turn your back on rude people without knowing a little more about them; they are often truthful and outspoken.

Do not reject unkind people, just because they have the courage to say "no".

Do not reject silent people as bores. They are often the most reliable friends.

And never respect negative virtues. A judge will never loiter with the intent to commit a felony and a thief will never pass a biased sentence from the bench; a millionaire will never steal a coat for his child, and an unemployed roadsweeper will never infringe the currency regulations during his holiday in Monte Carlo.

LIFE IN TECHNICOLOR

FINALLY, I wish to jot down a few revolutionary
suggestions.

What is the unit of humanity? Historians tell us that
it has varied throughout the ages: families, tribes and
city-states, national states and empires. Some people talk
of racial, others of religious units, others again create a
Western Union, dream of a United Europe and United
Asia. Professor Toynbee sees a civilisation as a unit.
I should like to remind people that the real but forgotten
unit of humanity. is man. Everything changes, but Mr.
Thomas Featherstone and Miss Elizabeth Walton are
eternal. I do not think of Mr. Featherstone or Miss
Walton as numbers on identity cards, staff numbers,
army numbers, national-health-service numbers, flat
numbers, telephone numbers, and library subscription
numbers. I think of Mr. Thomas Featherstone as a
chartered accountant who has rheumatism in his left leg,
supports the Arsenal, believes in spiritualism and is a
" compleat angler "; I think of Miss Elizabeth Walton as
a woman in love with an insurance clerk, who thinks she
speaks French, has a mania for buying hats and whose
favourite dish is jugged hare.

I think of men who, unlike heroes of modern novels,
do not kill anybody and are not killed by anybody. I
think of men who are not success-stories. Of course, it
is very nice to be an illiterate shoe-shine boy and become
the proprietor of a national daily or be a lovely girl and
make a wonderful marriage and be bored stiff for the
rest of her life, by an earl and not by a simple commoner.
But it is not bad either just to be born, to be educated,
to work, have a family, eat, read, travel, see nice paintings and buildings, listen to good music, meet people,

love and be loved, become the committee member of a golf club, the treasurer of a bridge club or become nothing at all in particular, and die in peace and be forgotten.

On our megaphones we can speak to vast crowds; on the radio to millions; in books to several hundreds of thousands of people; in our newspapers to whole nations; through films to the whole humanity. I am so proud. But what has happened to our conversation—when just one man faces another? What about our letters, written by one person to another? I know: "I received yours of the 12th inst. and thank you for the same." In jet-propelled aircraft we can travel at 700 m.p.h. But why not rediscover our walks in the sun at 2 m.p.h.?

Then I suggest that we should live our lives in Technicolor instead of in black and white. We are told that Mr. Krushchev is a great man, the British Parliament is a great institution, *War and Peace* is a great novel and Fascism is thoroughly bad. We tend to forget that besides black and white there are many brilliant and sublime colours—in fact, black and white are not colours at all. The British Parliamentary system may be—and I think it is—the best in the world, but it is infected with many foolish and atavistic customs and bonds. *War and Peace* is not only a great novel, but probably the greatest novel ever written, still it has unbearably tedious pages, chapters and parts. The Fascists, like all other dictators, were detestable, but—again like all other dictators—they had a mania for building, and that was certainly a good thing. Mr. Krushchev may be a great statesman, but I just could not believe—even if I were a subscriber to *Pravda*—that he is also a great general, a great admiral, a great economist, a great orator, the gentlest philanthropist, a great singer, an admirable athlete and a male beauty. Indiscriminate praise is one of the deadliest weapons any friends or admirers have ever forged against the victims of their admiration. I cannot see Krushchev black and white. I want to see him with his spots on.

I am very modest even in my dreams. I do not want to be a part of the manpower, I should like to be man; I do not want to be " housed ", I want a home; I do not want to eat calories, I want roast potatoes.

SHAKESPEARE
AND MYSELF

Introduction

THE first English writer whom I came to know intimately was William Shakespeare. I myself am the second.

There are certain differences between us which—in spite of the many books written about Shakespeare—have not been pointed out with sufficient clarity. He was born at Stratford-on-Avon, in the County of Warwick (England); I was born in Siklos, in the County of Baranya (Hungary). Very few outstanding English writers were born in Siklos—but not too many were born at Stratford, either.

As a successful English playwright, Shakespeare was second only to Ivor Novello. If I compare him with myself however—which seems inevitable—I find that almost all relevant points are in my favour. First, he wrote in archaic English which is often tiresome, while my language is absolutely up to the minute. (He cannot be blamed for this because he learned English earlier than I did; he was 2 when he learned it; I was 25.) Secondly, as a humorist, he belonged to rather a low class. He was a punster and he kept on cracking jokes. Cracking jokes should be below the dignity of any humorist who thinks something of himself. Jokes may be all right in tragedies and in any other kind of gloomy literature which needs light relief but they are quite out of place in serious humour. Thirdly, he was a hack. He turned out one play after the other for the commercial theatre, which kept him away from the kind of writing he was really keen on. "Business is business," he sighed bitterly and sat down to write Hamlet. He, like all sensitive souls, preferred cash to fame. But he acquired more fame than cash and that rankled more and more as he grew older.

The parallel between Shakespeare and myself, however, can be stretched too far. We are different kinds of writers. He was a playwright, I am a travel-book writer. He was always on the look-out for a soft job. He wrote about people of the past, people of ancient Rome and faraway Verona who presented no difficulties because nobody knew them. But I write about the English who are unfathomable and keep perplexing. It was easy for Shakespeare.

Very little is known about our lives. It is characteristic of the English that they turn out innumerable books on the life of Shakespeare—about whom it is almost impossible to find out anything—but not one single volume has been written about me, although I am just round the corner. It is true that I do not know much about my life either. I have forgotten many details, I mix up dates and facts and have never kept a diary. I thought of writing a letter to an editor: " Sir, I am engaged in a study of myself and I should be grateful to any of your readers for any kind of information." But I gave up the idea because people would send me facts, and facts are not only irrelevant but also misleading.

This book is not really a comparative study of myself and my late colleague. Enough has been said about him; and yet not enough. The whole world keeps on whining—if we only knew how Shakespeare worked, what he read, what he thought about his contemporaries and the price of beer. I must admit, I do not quite know what would happen in that case. Would beer be cheaper today or would Shakespeare be more interesting? Anyway, the same kind of complaint shall not be levelled against me. I cannot make up for deficiencies in knowledge concerning Shakespeare; but I shall not keep posterity on tenterhooks in the same way. I shall tell you everything, or almost everything about myself—how I live, how I work and what I think. But I shall refrain from saying anything about the price of beer. I cannot compete with Shakespeare in writing tragedies.

" Shakespeare and Myself "—I have called this book. It is a good but misleading title. If I have to choose between a good and an honest title, I always choose the good one. Here you have already an important clue to my character. The book is mostly about myself. As a motto, I shall keep to Francis Bacon's advice: " Praise yourself daringly, something always sticks."

G.M.

January, 1952.

PART I. *Personal*

ON BEING A WRITER

" WHAT on earth are you a writer for if you never write a book on Henry George?"

This question was put to me by a friend who is a dealer in postage-stamps, lives in Benghazi and spends all his free time composing quartets for wind instruments. In other words he is more obviously mad than most of us. I do not quite remember what reply I gave. But the first part of the question stuck in my mind: What on earth am I a writer for?

Next day or so I met another friend, a psychologist by profession. He, too, was more obviously mad than most of us. We met at a friend's house where we were having supper. I knew that he intended to leave soon after the meal because he had to fly to Luxembourg next day to visit his wife and that meant an early start. Still, I did not want to miss this opportunity and while we were having coffee in the lounge, I asked him as casually as I could:

" By the way, have you any idea why I became a writer?"

He was not surprised at all. Not only had he an idea but he was quite definite about it, as psychologists often are about most things. It was vanity, first of all; secondly, a streak of exhibitionism; thirdly, he said a number of nasty things about my subconscious which hurt me very badly because I hate my subconscious to be talked about in a disrespectful manner.

" Do you agree?" he asked me when he had finished his discourse.

" No," I said.

"And why not?" he asked rather aggressively.

" It would be no good telling you that I am no vainer

than the average commercial traveller. Nor would it be of any use to point out that I am not an exhibitionist but rather diffident and shy by nature. In reply, you would tell me a lot more disparaging things about my subconscious which I resent bitterly. And for all I know you may be right in this. But I still disagree with you because I know that if I were an actor or a politician and if I had asked you why I became an actor or a politician you would have answered in exactly the same terms, you would have spoken about vanity and exhibitionism, only changing your remarks about my subconscious a little to suit your explanation.''

" Very well,'' he said, standing up, " have you got a message ?''

" Yes.   Give my love to her.''

" I am not talking about my wife,'' he declared firmly. " Have you got a message for the world ?''

" Give my love to the world, too,'' I said.   Then somonee else joined us and we changed the subject.

I do not quite know whether his last question was to the point and whether it befitted a psychologist to ask it.   The question had never before occured to me.   On reflection, I do not think that I have message.   If I have—which I doubt—it was expressed in that silly answer to my friend: " Give my love to the world.''   Yes, I am a simple soul.   I wish I could get a little *Weltschmerz* from somewhere.   I wish I were a thin, pale poet, suffering all the tortures of mankind, instead of being a round-faced humorist, not suffering in the least.   I should love to brood over the future of humanity but it does not unduly worry me.   If humanity destroys itself, it will be regrettable but it will not be a catastrophe.   If humanity destroys itself, it will be a good lesson for the future and it will not do it again.   I have no illusions.   I know all the repulsive and ridiculous traits in my fellow human beings; I can study them in myself. But I still like good old humanity. And I feel a kind of patriotic love for our Earth although I dislike its snobbishness which makes it revolve around the Sun.   I do not see its future in bright colours but I cannot help loving the whole outfit. I am sorry but I cannot suffer like Strindberg and I have never eaten a pillow in my life.

Then why—I ask you, why—did I become a writer? Just because I did not know English? It is a good reason but not a compelling one.

It was difficult to find an explanation. I have to confess some painful facts about myself: ,

1. There is not one single person among my acquaintances so completely lacking in imagination as I am. I cannot make up a story and if someone else does, I find it utterly uninteresting. I am very fond of many novels but there is not a single one among them for the story of which I care a rap.

2. I am so uneducated that I often astonish myself. It is true, I have one rather unusual gift: I can get fairly well acquainted with almost any subject at an amazing speed, just to forget it equally quickly. There are not a dozen flowers I know; I do not recognise any birds, except pigeons, ostriches and polar bears—and the third on my list is not even a bird. As I was not brought up in England, I could not make up for all the deficiencies in my education and I have never read a single line by such authors as George Meredith or Henry James. There is not one single subject under the sun I am expert on. You may mention anything you like and I can tell you confidently beforehand that I know nothing about it; or worse than nothing, just a little. I am interested in the Latin language, in grammars in general, mathematics and law. But not even on these am I an expert. I am one of the most uneducated people I have ever met.

3. I have no desire to save or change the world. I cannot offer you a new moral code although I am not exactly enamoured of the old one; I cannot offer you a new philosophy. I have a great admiration for philosophers but it always seems to me, when I read anyone from Heraclitus through Thomas Aquinas to William James, that there is an easily noticeable gap in every system and the philosophers argue themselves to a deadlock and pretend not to notice the gap. But I do not even have a system; I only have the gap.

Except pigeons, ostriches and polar bears

There is one point which does offer an explanation. I love writing. Not too much writing at a time but I love it. It amuses me. Not that I can laugh my head off at my own works; in fact, I never look at a book of mine after it is published. No, it is not the result which gives me pleasure but the actual writing. Why it should be so, I cannot tell. It is hard work, rather harder than chopping wood.

I think I am just the eternal writer who never creates anything worth while and has no other merit than that he (and another few hundred thousand) keeps literature alive. A man who has nothing to say but has an irresistible urge to say it.

ON BEING A HUMORIST

A GREAT deal of responsibility and blame for my becoming a humorist must be attached to *The Times Literary Supplement*. I know this is a libellous statement but I hope that thanks to the proposed new libel laws I might get away with an apology.

In 1945 a book of mine, called *We Were There to Escape* was published. It was one of the first escape stories to be written and—because of publishing delays—one of the last to appear during the war. It was the story of a Serbian Captain and was narrated in the first person singular. I received a few good reviews and others patted me on the back. I, quite rightly, regarded the book as the work of a reporter and not of a writer. I put down on paper what the Captain had told me in a number of long interviews, because I thought his story worth telling and probably also because I needed money—a not altogether unusual incentive and source of artistic inspiration. But I must have deviated from the rules of straight reporting without being aware of my deviationist tendencies. It was *The Times Literary Supplement* which brought home this fact to me. Its review began :

" There is a peculiar kind of Slav humour," (why Slav I still do not know.) " It came out delightfully in Capek's work —and all through this narrative it is more or less present. Even without it, the story would be one of the best that has come out of the war ... It is something new in the way of escapes from P.O.W. camps and is full of thrills and exciting adventures. With humour added, it has the light touch that turns unpleasant and indeed horrifying experience into good reading. Even the appaling monotony of camp life ... is presented in a comic light."

This was a very important review for me. Of course, I was pleased with the praise but this was the less significant part of it. I was somewhat shattered by the fact that the book had been called humorous. I was not aware of its being funny in the least. I thought it was a thriller pure and simple, rather in the style of *War and Peace* and the *Odyssey*. If you can imagine Tolstoy receiving reviews after the appearance of *War and Peace* stating that his book was a pretty piece of fun, or if you can picture Homer, hearing that his epic poems were good examples of a peculiar brand of Slav humour, then you can imagine my feelings.

After some heart-searching, I was driven to the conclusion that I might as well attempt to write something, which it would not cause me painful surprise to find described as humorous. One phrase especially reverberated in my memory: " . . . the light touch that turns unpleasant, indeed horrifying, experiences into good reading." I sat down and told all about my unpleasant, indeed, horrifying, experiences among the English.

That book, *How to be an Alien*, and its successors, have put a label on me. Now I am a humorist and I cannot get out of it. I am not complaining. I dislike the clown who wants to play Hamlet; and I dislike, even more, the clown who acts as if he were Hamlet in disguise, because his teachings are more readily accepted if served up in a humorous form. I am no teacher; I have never felt that I could offer much wisdom to anybody. I am a plain reporter, rather on the dry side. I have described people and things as I saw them and naturally I could not help describing them as *I* saw them. If Sophocles had come to England in 1938 as a correspondent of a Greek paper—as I did as correspondent of a Hungarian one—he would have written a tragedy about his experiences and by today the Complex of Not Being English would rank equally with the Oedipus Complex. I have no complex because I have not got a deep soul. My soul has width and length but it entirely lacks depth. I have written books on the English, on foreigners, on the Americans, on the Jews and the Communists. If these books happened to be funny, it is due to the fact that *they* are funny, not I. People call me a humorist in self-defence. If I am not a humorist, they must all be rather silly. And of course it suits them better that I should be silly rather than they. Very well, it suits me too.

What kind of animal, then, is a humorist ? There are two kinds of humorists: the humorous humorists and the non-humorous humorists. The humorous humorists keep cracking jokes and are anxious to be funny. But good humour is not an ability to describe things in a " funny light "—i.e. to pretend that things are what they are not; it is an ability to see things as they really are and not as they pretend to be. Humour is not a joke; it is just a way of looking at things.

Mr. Wodehouse is an example of the humorous humorist. I read his books—one in three years—and tears run down my cheeks. I roar with laughter; I shriek with laughter; I laugh till I can laugh no more. Then I put the book down with a yawn, feeling that I have been bored stiff. Aristophanes and Stephen Leacock, on the other hand, are deadly serious. They describe things as they see them just as Picasso paints things as he sees them. The result may be ridiculous in all these cases, but the vision is a true one.

Or take Mr. Evelyn Waugh. He is an excellent, indeed I believe a great writer, so long as he expresses himself in a manner which is natural to him. *The Loved One* for example was a little masterpiece, probably his best work. In *Brideshead Revisited* and in *Helena* he tried to be serious. In fact, he only started walking on his feet which is as unnatural for him as it would be for many others to stand on their heads. This unusual angle impairs and dulls his vision. I laughed at every page of *The Loved One* and felt at the end that a shattering and terrifying picture of our modern civilisation had been revealed to me; I read *Brideshead Revisited* and found it pompous, snobbish and over-written. I had the feeling sometimes that Mr. Waugh was caricaturing the style of someone he rather dislikes. Mr. Waugh should not stand on his feet; it must be too tiring for him. But I understand his case perfectly well. A humorist is forced into a pigeonhole and frequently adjured by his publishers and readers never to leave it. Whereupon he starts feeling

Shrieked with laughter

Bored stiff

fidgety. His pigeonhole becomes his prison and his cage, and he feels he must rebel and break out. He claims his right to be dull and turns out his own *Hamlet*. He is tired of being a lightweight and decides to take part in heavyweight competitions. He may try, of course, but he should not be surprised when he knocks himself out by his own well-delivered punches.

Most humorists have one great advantage over other people.

When others are bored or infuriated, I am usually amused. When an excruciating bore is present from whom others flee as from a leper, I usually spend a delightful hour with him and encourage him to talk. In the United States—when I went out to write a book on that country—I encountered certain phenomena which drove others mad with fury; I rubbed my hands with glee and made notes busily. When I found something quite normal, I was disappointed; when I listened to their radio programmes, I was overjoyed. Life for others is life; for me it is raw material. I know of course that if someone kicks a humorist in the . . . well, anywhere, it will hurt him exactly as it hurts other people. But the humorist sits down after a while, writes down his experiences in a distorted form in which he is either the hero or the maltreated victim, whereupon he feels all square with the world. I do not quite know why this should give us satisfaction but it does. Writing keeps us from more criminal activities. A new work is our just revenge on the world.

ON NOT KNOWING ENGLISH

WHATEVER one may think of my works, one must admit that they are not too bad for a child of fourteen. Because, as an English writer, I am fourteen years old.

When I was sent to England in 1938 I thought I knew English fairly well. In Budapest my English proved quite sufficient. I could get along with it. On arrival in this country, I found that Budapest English was quite different from London English. I should not like to seem biased, but I found Budapest English much better in many ways.

In England I found two difficulties. First: I did not understand people and secondly: they did not understand me. It was easier with written texts. Whenever I read a leading article in *The Times*, I understood everything perfectly well except that I could never make out whether *The Times* was for or against something. In those days I put this down to my lack of knowledge of English.

The first step in my progress was when people started understanding me while I still could not understand them. This was the most talkative period of my life. Trying to hide my shortcomings, I kept on talking, keeping the conversation as unilateral as possible. I reached the stage of intelligibility fairly quickly, thanks to a friend of mine who discovered an important linguistic secret, namely that the English mutter and mumble. Once we noticed a sausage-like thing in a shop-window, marked PORK BRAWN. We mistook it for a Continental kind of sausage and decided to buy some for our supper. We entered the shop and I said: "A quarter of pork brawn please." "What was that?"—asked the shopkeeper looking scared. "A quarter of pork brawn please"—I repeated, still with a certain nonchalance. I repeated it again. I repeated it a dozen times with no success. I talked slowly and softly; I shouted; I talked in the way one talks to the mentally deficient; I talked as one talks to the deaf and finally I tried baby-talk. The shopkeeper still had no idea whether we wanted to buy or sell something. Then my friend had a brain-wave. " Leave it to me"—he said in Hungarian and started mumbling under his nose in a hardly audible and quite unintelligible manner. The shopkeeper's eyes lit up: " I see"—he said happily—"you want a quarter of pork brawn. Why didn't you say so ?" —Yes, that was the solution. I never uttered an intelligible sentence until I learnt English fairly well; and not too many after that, either.

The next stage was that I began to understand foreigners but not the English or the Americans. The more atrocious a foreign accent someone had, the clearer he sounded to me. I remember that as a child I used to be very much annoyed at not being able to read. My irritation led me finally to develop a theory: I firmly believed that no-one could read at all. I was convinced that grown-ups could not really read; they only acted as though they could, to keep up an otherwise badly tarnished reputation of superiority before us children. I had long forgotten my theory of general illiteracy but in my early years in London I was reminded of it. Once sitting in a news-cinema, I was particularly irritated by not understanding one single word of the commentator. The whole commentary —probably delivered in American—struck me as an avalanche of undistinguishable vocal noises. Not that I did not know the words: I was sure that I knew quite a number of them, but I could not spot any familiar words at all. I sighed to myself: " Good heavens ! Will there be, can there be, a time when I shall understand all this ?" Then my childhood suspicion reoccurred to me. I felt convinced that no-one else understood a word; I was absolutely certain that no-one could possibly get anything out of this tornado of nasal muttering. I firmly believed that the whole thing was a put-up job, just to fool me. Good old days ! Today I sit in the news cinema, listening to the American commentator, thinking of the past days with longing and sighing to myself : "Good Heavens ! Was there, could there be, a time when I did not understand all this ?"

It was quite constructive to see how all of us, newly arrived Hungarians, picked up exactly the kind of English we needed. I had been in London for a few months when a friend of mine, an actor of the Hungarian National Theatre, arrived here on holiday. He played with the idea of staying here but eventually he returned to Budapest. After having spent about two days sight-seeing with me he suddenly asked me on the escalator of a tube station:

" Tell me, is there an actor here in London by the name of Noel Coward ? "

" There must be one "—I replied—" because I think I read one of his plays in a Hungarian translation."

" That's him "—my friend nodded. " He says he is also a playwright."

He told me that having met Mr. Coward in Paris, he had promised to ring him up in London. To be compelled to talk English on the telephone was still a nightmare to me. But not to my friend. He walked to the telephone booth, entered it, took a tiny notebook out of his pocket, looked up the number and rang up Mr. Coward. My friend knew about a dozen words in English but his French was not half so good. Yet, Coward and he had some 45 minutes animated conversation in Norman English—I mean a strange mixture of English and French—bursting out laughing twice every minute. Next day he went to visit Mr. Coward and he went on seeing him fairly regularly for some time. I, too, went along once or twice and was terribly shy, stupid and timid. But my actor friend was the centre of attraction. As a wit he put Mr. Coward in the shade and many of the ladies fell in love with him.

He had an amazing ability for picking up set phrases and remembering full sentences he had heard. He was unable to put together three words without making half a dozen grammatical mistakes, but if he repeated something he had heard from the others he did not have a trace of foreign accent. He sounded as if he had just come down from Oxford. I regarded this as cheating. But he, being an actor, obviously concentrated his abilities on pronunciation. Soon I noticed

Terribly shy

that I was cheating, too, but in my own way. I preferred corresponding with people to talking to them. I could pick up and memorise written phrases and was able to concoct quite acceptable letters while in speech I still sounded a savage. And so it was with all of us. Commercial travellers picked up their own English with incredible ease and I had a friend who could write a brilliant essay on the most complicated legal subject while he was still unable to order a portion of Gorgonzola cheese, let alone a blancmange, in a restaurant.

Looking back today my own courage—to write in English for English readers—makes me shiver. No, it was not courage, it was reckless audacity. I did not quite realise what I was trying to do. I shall never regret that I learned English as a grown-up. Of course, there are great gaps in my knowledge but I have one consolation. I am much more aware of the beauties of the English language than quite a few Englishmen.

I should like to mention only one characteristic of the English language which exasperated me at first but which I now find delightful.

In English, the order of words follows very strict rules from which you cannot depart. If you do, your sentence loses not only its beauty and grace but also its sense. The result is that, in acceptable English, you can be stupid but you cannot be obscure. And this simple rule about the order of words was the death warrant for many Continental giants. In German—to mention one Continental language fairly well known here—you can write ponderous sentences, each two yards long, with a string of verbs at the end. It may sound impressive, profound and pregnant with ideas. Translate it into English and it is unmasked. If it has something to say, it will say it; if it has nothing to say it will resemble that pompous and conceited King of the fable who rode through his capital, thinking that he was wearing magnificent regal robes while he was, in fact, stark naked. The English, it is said, are not prone to become dogmatic. How could they? Most dogmas and theories when translated into English lose their mythical haze and enigmatic charm and sound plain silly.

There was a time when I tended to become very proud of my knowledge of English. Luckily, every now and then one goes through a sobering experience which teaches one to be more humble. Not very long ago my mother came here from Hungary on a visit. She expressed her wish to take English lessons at an L.C.C. class, which some of her friends attended. I accompanied her to the school and we were received by a commissionaire. I enquired about the various classes and said that we were interested in the class for beginners. I received all the neccessary information and conducted a lengthy conversation with the man, in the belief that my English sounded vigorous and idiomatic. In the end, I paid out the fees for my mother. He looked at me with astonishment and asked: "What? Only one? And what about you?"

ON BEING NEITHER HERE NOR THERE

ABOUT six years ago I felt that I had been recognised as an English writer. It was my dentist who recognised me. He was a morose and taciturn kind of Englishman whom I had to see often in those days. After my tenth visit he felt that he knew me intimately enough to ask me what my profession was.

" I am a journalist and a writer," I replied.

A long pause followed, then he remarked:

" I have another patient who also says that he is a writer."

" What's his name ?" I asked.

" Maugham. A man by the name of Somerset Maugham."

" Oh . . . " I exclaimed.

" Do you know him ?"

" No, I don't know him," I replied.

" Then why did you say *oh* ?"

I gave no satisfactory explanation but asked him what kind of a man Mr. Somerset Maugham was. He thought again, then summed him up:

" Not so talkative as you."

I was very proud of that. The feeling that at least in the mind of one person I was pictured as "one of the two writers," the other being Mr. Maugham, gave me the satisfactory feeling that I had arrived somewhere.

But soon afterwards I started realising that I was neither here nor there.

In England—I thought—I would always remain a foreigner. I was quite prepared to die for King and country—should it be really necessary but that was an unimportant aspect of the matter. I knew that I should never like beans on toast; that I should never spend delightful hours snail-watching; that I should never be really entertaining in conversations kept strictly to the "glorious day isn't it " line. I live behind Lords Cricket Ground and can hear the cheers of the crowd in my flat but I remained certain that I should never know whether a man who takes four wickets for nineteen runs and twelve maidens, has done something laudable or something very naughty indeed. I would be—I felt fairly sure—a tall, lean and taciturn Englishman, smoking a pipe and trimming hedges on Saturday afternoons.

But when I went back to Hungary in 1948, I did not find myself at home there either. I looked at my former compatriots through the eyes of the worst kind of Blimp. I found most of them loud, boastful, inquisitive, ill-mannered, quickwitted, well-informed and intelligent. A bunch of blooming foreigners, in short. The Duke of Wellington returning to England after the Peninsular War, could not have exclaimed more happily: "At home again!" than I did, returning from Hungary. Yes, I felt happy and at home until I heard that the laundries had raised their charges by one penny in the shilling. It was not so much the actual increase that worried me; but what a way of putting it! Why couldn't they say that they had raised their charges by 8% or 10%. But if they had said it hardly anybody would have understood what the increase meant. What a country!— I sighed.

Then, for a long time I thought I should remain an eternal exile. An " eternal exile " sounds rather good. It was a nice, heroic pose. But I soon get fidgety in nice, heroic poses, I can never wear them with dignity. " Why should I be an eternal exile ?" I asked myself. From the first minute I set foot in England I had felt myself almost at home and had got on very well with English people. At first perhaps even better than later. I had been able to appreciate their kindness, straight-forwardness and civilised ways and not knowing their language, I thought them brilliant, too. (Having no common language with them helps you immensely in conversation with the English.) I remembered that during my first five years or so in this country it had never occurred to me that I was an exile. I had felt quite normal. Why

Never be an Englishman

should this idea get hold of me soon after my naturalisation when, in fact, I had ceased to be an exile ?

The explanation slowly dawned on me. I felt an exile in England because I was getting perfectly anglicised. A dreary thought, but there I was. All the English feel like exiles at home. They always speak softly, not because they are well-behaved, but because they do not feel quite at home. They set foot on the Continent and are louder than the French. The stiffness of their manners at home is the stiffness of visitors who cannot quite get used to the place in 30, 50 or 70 years. They have no uproarious rows, even in politics, not because they are not temperamental enough, but because you must feel really at home to make a healthy row. The English are in a pub, the political parties standing round the bar, glasses in hand and eyeing one another calmly and with cold suspicion: who is going to pay for the next round ? Yes, at last I found the explanation: I felt an exile because I had arrived home.

MY POSITION IN WORLD LITERATURE

I WISH I were second rate. Unfortunately, I cannot claim that distinction.

Think of the great novelists. If Homer (I count him as the first great novelist), Tolstoy, Dostoevsky, Balzac, Cervantes and Dickens are first rate, then Stendhal, Flaubert and Proust are second rate. I should classify Gorky and Thackeray as third rate, Wells, Arnold Bennett and Joseph Conrad fourth rate, Maupassant as fifth, Galsworthy as sixth rate, G.B. Shaw (as a novelist) about tenth rate and many excellent and distinguished present-day novelists as twelfth rate. Make the same classification with playwrights. If Sophocles, Shakespeare, Molière, Ibsen and Shaw are first rate (I am not counting " Faust " as a play), then Schiller is second rate and Bridie eighth rate. Or take poets: if Horace, Shakespeare, Goethe, Baudelaire, Keats and Shelley are first rate, then Byron is second rate and Housman tenth rate. I know, of course, that I shall not find one single reader who agrees with my actual classification but that is entirely beside the point. He can make his own and if he strictly adheres to the rules—i.e. to put authors of different value into different categories—he will find that a twelfth rate author is still a giant. In fact, I have omitted the names of living writers from my list; if you include them in yours, you will find that to be called twenty-fourth rate still means real distinction.

I have just read a book of literary criticism by Edmund Wilson. He likes calling a number of authors (Mr. Somerset Maugham among them) second rate. He uses this adjective in a derogatory sense. I hold Mr. Maugham in much higher esteem than Mr. Wilson does—maybe, because I have read his works and he has not—but I should call him seventh rate because he really is very good. Mr. Wilson himself is an excellent critic. A genuine ninth-rater—and that says a great deal for him.

I think such a classification is quite justified, especially in an age in which, for instance, "hundred per cent." has become an accepted adjective in the measurement of literary values. My way of ranking literary achievement is fairer than any other. It is a pity, of course, that we cannot weigh writers as we can boxers. To talk of Bantamweight and Welterweight writers would sound rather attractive.

Taking the foregoing literary principles into consideration, I should like to fix my place in world literature. Nobody else is anxious to do it, so I must not shrink from the task. I hope you will not regard me as too conceited if I call myself fourteenth rate. I know, I am flying high but I have my self-esteem and cannot forget the fact that I am somewhat immortal. Or as it is fashionable to put it nowadays: not entirely un-immortal. "Immortal" has never been an absolute term. A literary creation may live a few thousand years—that's all. There are about 17,000 books published yearly in England alone. Most of them die within a few months. Any book which lives for a year has achieved a measure of immortality. A bit of immortality; a spot of immortality; a short-term immortality if you like—but immortality all the same. I know that many authors are considerably more immortal than I am but I am fairly immortal myself. If I do not physically survive my own literary immortality I shall be content.

In England, however, you cannot easily outlive your fame. This is a great danger in other countries, but not here. In England the author who reaches his seventy-fifth birthday is quite safe.

My own literary future depends on one question: how long shall I live? In other countries a writer who reaches the age of seventy-five is considered an old writer; in England he is considered a great writer. If one keeps on writing—no matter what—for five decades, one's place in literature is assured.

After fifty years of sustained literary production not only the writer's faults and vices are forgiven but even his virtues and greatness. Take the example of three eminent

men. Bernard Shaw was considered a pagan revolutionary whose name was not to be uttered in good company. Bertrand Russell was even worse because he is an earl and it is much more difficult to forgive an earl than an Irishman. Mr. Somerset Maugham was, in the past, always described as a superficial entertainer. Today they are—or Shaw was, until recently—the great old men of English literature. They have not changed but they have held out. I could mention ten others who have no merits other than old age. Yet, everybody admires—not their great age and good health—but their literary achievements.

After a certain time they become a tradition and a habit. And the English always prefer a bad tradition to a good writer.

If I prove successful, I may die as young as I like; but if I fail I should like to reach the happy state of senility and idiocy. I am not without my ambitions.

ON THE GLORY OF COFFEE HOUSES

I HAVE travelled a fair amount. I have seen Red Indians in North America and exotic tribal chiefs in Asia; I have seen half-savage shepherd-poets in the Balkans and nomadic lawyers in Israel. But the greatest change I have ever experienced was between the literary climate of Budapest and the literary climate of London.

After my matriculation, I was sent to Vienna for a year to learn German. The older generation which grew up in the Austrian-Hungarian Empire knew German as well as they knew Hungarian. But I started going to school after World War I, and my generation took almost as great a pride in not knowing German as one might justifiably take in knowing Chinese perfectly. We looked down upon people who knew German; it was not patriotic. By the time I was eighteen, this mood had passed and I was sent to Vienna but never learnt German really well. Instead, I picked up a working knowledge of Russian from Lithuanian girls but I have forgotten that, too.

Returning to Budapest where we then lived, I told my family that I wanted to become a writer and a journalist. I had already got a small job for myself on a Sunday paper. My mother opposed my decision as strongly as she could oppose anything. She wanted me to study law (my father and grandfather were lawyers). In the end she agreed that I should try to work as a journalist too, but I was to get along with my university studies. " One can be a gentleman and a journalist at the same time," my mother said, since she knew very little of journalism. She reconciled herself with my decision to a certain extent because—as she often explained—journalism was an excellent springboard to everything: politics or a legal career. I always maintained that I had no desire to spring; I did not wish to achieve success in one field to utilise it in another. I regarded that as treachery. I wanted to become a journalist and later a writer, too, which meant the same category of undesirables to my family. In fairness to my mother, she would not have minded seeing me a Nobel Prize winner ; but she liked me and liked books much too much to wish to see me a hack. But, unfortunately, I could not give any binding promise concerning the Nobel Prize.

Eventually I got my degree. I became a " doctor of law " as almost every middle class person became a doctor of something in Central Europe at that time. I had been studying feverishly to get my university years over. I could not help falling in love with the Law and I have kept up a flirtation with the legal sciences ever since. By the time I received my degree I had progressed far enough in journalism and even my mother knew that there was no hope of my remaining (or rather becoming) a gentleman. I had been a reporter, a writer of feature articles, and later a theatre and film critic. I loved my work and took it seriously. I wished to discuss every musical comedy in the terms of Lessing's " Hamburgische Dramaturgie " and on the principles of Pal Gyulai, the great Hungarian critic.

Yes, I was a proper and acknowledged writer and journalist. One could tell that by the coffee houses I visited and the tables I sat at in those cafés.

The greatest single contribution of the late lamented Austro-Hungarian Empire to human civilisation was the coffee-house. The farther West you travelled, the more the coffee houses lost their Central European character. The French café is still a wonderful institution but not quite the same as the establishments of Budapest or Vienna. England, of course, is just a barbaric place without coffee houses. It has been often pleaded in defence that England did not need any coffee houses. This may be true but even if it is, it does not exonerate England of the charge. You cannot say: X, is not a barbarian because he does not even *need* a toothbrush.

In Budapest you could find a coffee house on every street corner. That was a peculiarity of Budapest architecture. You went in and ordered a glass of black coffee which cost you about a shilling in the best coffee houses and much less in more modest establishments. For this sum, (a) you were entitled to sit at a table, for an indefinite period, all alone, occupying a very comfortable arm-chair; (b) waiters came and gave you fresh glasses of water every half hour; (c) you were given all the newspapers and periodicals—Hungarian and foreign; (d) if you wanted to, you were given pen and ink and you could write there—as in fact most Hungarian writers actually did. Of course you could also eat in the coffee houses —have breakfast, lunch and dinner there and many of them kept open day and night. So if you wished you could spend there 24 hours, 24 days or 24 years on end. A colleague of mine who worked on the same paper as I did, once met a well known poet on a Wednesday afternoon in a coffee house and they decided to play Casino—the fashionable card-game of the day. They went on playing till Saturday midday when my colleague stood up and said that he was sorry but now he had to leave for the weekly conference in our editorial office. The poet's face darkened. He looked at the scores, threw the sum he had lost at his opponent, and declared with deep contempt: " You ought to have told me you were in a hurry." The most important thing was, however, the character of the café you visited. Each café belonged to a certain trade, profession or sect. There were coffee houses frequented by writers, others by lawyers or furniture-merchants, university professors, horse dealers, landowners, thieves, diplomatists, card-sharpers, actors, members of parliament or prostitutes. All this was highly specialised. Politicians belonging to different wings of the same party would not visit the same coffee house; an ordinary thief would not visit the café frequented by pickpockets and an actor would not sit at the table of music-hall artists. There was a strict hierarchy in the coffee houses visited by prostitutes. The aristocracy of that profession was even more snobbish than the aristocracy of most others. If a card-sharper changed his trick, he had to change his coffee house, too. It was one of the secret and mysterious laws of Budapest life that you were bound to find your appropriate coffee house and that

Twenty-four years on end . . . .

you appropriate coffee house was bound to find you. You could go up and down on the social or professional ladder and as your luck changed so changed your coffee house, too. That is why a Budapest coffee house was a much more exclusive place than the most exclusive English club. There no members were elected for life. And not only those were compelled to leave who had sunk too low but those who had ascended too high. And that is where the real exclusivity begins.

People knew which coffee house you were to be found in. They addressed letters there for you and they rang you up on the telephone. The newspaper-boy knew which papers you were interested in and he brought them to you—English dailies, Swedish weeklies or Dutch chess journals—as soon as you settled down. The waiters were your friends. They were not chummy, of course, in fact, they were much too polite for my liking. The head-waiter—the man who presented the bill and took your money—was usually your banker, too. He allowed you an overdraft in the form of credit and often lent you money and gave you tips for the horse-races. In one of the literary coffee houses the head-waiter lent enormous sums to writers and poets whose works he liked. He lost more money on writers than most publishers. Nor did he grudge it, either. (It is true that in spite of this he retired a rich man, immortalised in many beautiful poems and famous short stories by his defaulting creditors.)

These coffee houses were intellectual centres, the like of which is not to be found here. Clubs or pubs are in a different world. In Central Europe all political and literary movements started in coffee houses and often emerged from casual conversations. Even revolutions started in cafés. The 1848 revolution—which soon developed into a war of freedom against Austria and excited and animated the whole world for two years—originated from the Café Pilvax. Great events in the first 900 years of Hungarian history were all connected with battlefields; great events of the last century were all connected with Budapest cafés.

Central Europeans congregated in coffee houses because they wanted to meet those of like interests and because they loved talking. They went to coffee houses because there they could talk; the English go to their Clubs because they must keep quiet there. The first law of English social life is that you must not talk; the second, that if you must talk you should not talk of anything which may possibly interest you or the other fellow. The English rightly believe that interesting topics are often vulgar. So what? In Budapest cafés, very little was said about the weather. The conversation was often incredibly and shamefully indiscreet. People appeared and told you that they had just come from this or that lady's bed. (It must be mentioned to their honour, that they were just as often lying as not.) The conversation was so personal that having spent fourteen years in England, I sometimes doubt my memory whether it ever really occurred. The permanent debate was loud, vulgar, personal and cruel; but it was witty, interesting, inspiring and well informed, too. The coffee house was a queer mixture of the Agora of ancient Athens, a Temple of Ideas and a spiritual brothel. It was the gregarious instinct which herded us together; we teased, indeed, tortured one another but were there because we longed for the warmth which the crowd generates. And, of course, we gathered together day by day, because we also wanted to keep an eye on each other. The natural instinct of the Enlish is to keep to themselves. That is why they leave their homes and congregate in clubs. A club is a place where a few hundred Englishmen can be alone. The best literary, legal and political brains in the country assemble, sit down and remain silent on the burning questions of the day.

ON THE LACK OF COFFEE HOUSES

WHAT kind of literature was born, or, at least, conceived in Budapest on those round café-tables of imitation marble?

The world knows a great deal of Hungarian literature or rather of certain Hungarian literary products which became famous or notorious. There was a time, before the last war, when Hungarian farces and light comedies flooded the stages of Europe (except the London stage). They were manufactured on the conveyor belt. Literary factories sprang up, with proper planning boards and managements, play-designers, dialogue-men, gag-men, finishers, etc. A team or six or eight literary stakhanovites turned out these successful plays in scores. There is little to boast about in this. There is little to boast about in the incredible number of motion picture experts—screen-writers, directors, producers—which Hungary gave to the world. Few of them were artists of any standing, few were even decent craftsmen. One or two made their mark but most of them only proved that there was some affinity between the spirit of Budapest and the spirit of Hollywood, at their worst. The superficial cleverness and enchanting arrogance of the Budapest boulevards mixed well with those English and American business-men who occupied the strategic points in the important suburbs of culture Hungarian gag-merchants, dialogue-dealers, second-hand story-mongers, plot-repairers, episode-retailers and " I make your old jokes look like new men," occupied so many key-positions in Hollywood and London that—according to one story—large notices were put up in the leading Hollywood film offices : " It is not enough to be Hungarian."

Behind this rather shallow export of persons and goods there was a Hungarian literature, rich and admirable and quite out of proportion to the smallness of the country and the isolation of the language. Modern Hungarian novelists, generally speaking, were not outstanding but the essayists, both light and serious, were superb. In the short story they shone and glittered and there were a few plays really worth seeing that never reached the international market. But, first of all, there were in the last hundred years some four Hungarian poets who would rank among the greatest in the world if only the world could understand them.

The nation is small and its language isolated, consequently Hungarian literature is considerably poorer and considerably richer than English. Poorer because, obviously, it could not produce so much and on such a level; but also richer because all the masterpieces of the world are available in superb translations. Translation is a horror in England; it is a word of almost magic power in small countries. In England, a first class poet or writer will hardly touch translation work; in Hungary (and in all the small countries) the best poets and writers vie with one another in translating the great works of foreign literature (Germany and Russia must also be counted on this score among the small countries.) There are some excellent translators in England, too, but Shakespeare or Shaw or Keats would never have dreamt of spending their time translating foreign poetry. The Hungarians and Swedes and Portuguese have different ideas. They know foreign languages to start with—a not altogether insignificant factor in this case. Arany, one of the great geniuses of Hungarian poetry translated three of Shakespeare's plays—and these translations are worthy of the originals in all respects. But who on earth would or could translate Arany into English? Or into any language, for that matter? And if someone didtranslate him into English, who would bother to read him ?

It was Alexander Hevesi, a former director of the Hungarian National Theatre who used to tell me in one of the Budapest cafés, a great deal about the problems of translation. Arany had translated *Hamlet, A Midsummer's Night Dream* and *King John,* but then he was persuaded by some of his friend to give up Shakespeare and pick up Aristophanes instead. He did in fact translate almost all of Aristophanes' plays. Now,

not even Hevesi would have ventured to speak ill of
Aristophanes in my presence because he is one of my favourite
humorous writers; but even I had to admit that Aristophanes
was no Shakespeare. Hevesi was in despair when he
remembered that we might have had all Shakespeare's plays
translated by Arany but for the interference of some fools
and busybodies. Speaking of this subject, he—rather a quiet
man with great self-control—used to grow purple with rage
and get worked up into quite a personal anger against Arany's
idiotic advisers—although all this had happened about
eighty years before. Hevesi himself was not only one of the
outstanding theatrical producers and theoreticians of the
drama but also a playwright and translator of high standing.
He translated all Shaw's works, produced them in the National
Theatre and was just such an ardent prophet of both Ibsen
and Shaw in Hungary as, for instance, Shaw was of Ibsen in
this country. Whenever Hevesi came to London, he stayed
partly with the Granville Barkers and partly with the Shaws.
When I left for London, he gave me a warm introductory
letter to Bernard Shaw—but I did not dare to use it. I did
not know English and I thought a visit to Shaw would be
rather an impertinent waste of his time. I could not have
been a visitor, I should have been a sightseer. Later, when I
wanted to go, I could not find the letter.

(This last reminiscence is just one story of my planned
autobiography: How I missed meeting the greatest person-
alities of our age.)

I have mentioned at least one specific subject of our table
talk: Hevesi discoursing on the art of poetic and dramatic
translation. But what is the conversation of writers in
England ?

First of all, there is no such thing. I admit, I may have
met the wrong kind of writers—although I have met many;
it is also possible that they talk differently to me than to
others because I am a humorist. Almost everybody tries to
be witty and jocular with a humorist because a humorist is
a funny man and they wish to prove that they know how to

Shavian Sightseer

treat such a fellow. At the same time the humorist himself is solemn or pompous, trying to prove that in spite of being only a humorist, he is a serious man full of deep thoughts and emotions. The only subject which—according to my experience —can rouse a modern English writer, is the subject of royalties and income tax. If a modern Boswell were to set down the conversation of the great literary artists of this age, the result would be an efficient " Plain Man's Guide to Income Tax."

Writers are not interested in politics and if they are, their conception hardly ever rises above the leading article standard of the popular dailies. Naturally, they refuse to talk of literature too, because to be interested in literature has an "amateurish" touch. They are interested in the Cup Final, in the Test Matches, but primarily in Income Tax. I am not speaking now of journalists who, generally speaking, are much better; nor of specialists, historians and academic people who write books. I am talking of writers proper and I find eight out of ten incredibly dull.

Do not believe for a moment that I wish to discuss the art of translation, and the works of Aristophanes with everyone I meet. I am delighted to listen to good stories; I enjoy discussing common acquaintances (and pulling them to pieces) and do not mind at all if I am supplying food for similar conversation in my absence or even in my presence; I am prepared to listen to anyone speak on any subject he knows something about or is, at least, interested in; I am quite happy talking nonsense, or arguing about cooking, shopping and even about income tax. In fact, I hate artificial and affected talk on arts. But I do find the small talk of English literary men dreary and uninspired. They can stutter without speaking a word; they can get confused without uttering a sound; they can be almost as dull keeping silent as they are when talking. A rare feat.

I have many amusing and intelligent friends with whom I can talk to my heart's delight; journalists, some artists, radio-people, porters, garage-men, business-men and a milkman. (The trouble with business-men is that they often insist on discussing poetry and their souls while I am interested in finance and the money-market.) Yes, I have many dear and intimate friends. I have noticed, by the way, that people, generally speaking, talk in a freer and more unreserved fashion to me than to English-born people. My foreign accent does not raise class-barriers: a foreigner does not belong to any class, he's a foreigner. People are always prepared to be more communicative and open hearted to me than to one of themselves because it does not really matter what I know and think about them. I have heard the confessions of many; I have been consulted by dozens; I have discussed intimate problems with hosts of people of all ranks and stations. But I have not met more than five writers in England with whom I could spend half an hour without being bored stiff.

What is the reason for this? English writers are socially displaced persons, and almost all feel a little frustrated. We live in a puritanic, bourgeois society and our profession is neither puritanical nor bourgeois. Journalists, actors and even dramatists are better off: they, fortunately for themselves, are forced to live in their own circles, mix mostly with one another and—by tacit understanding—accept their own moral code. Writers, however, behave as if they had accepted my mother's maxim: " One can be a writer and a gentleman at the same time." They accept the business-men's standard in a business-men's community. They all want to be respectable. They do not feel that they form a class of their own and to enter any other class would mean loss of status for them. Their main dream is a settled bank account—not for the sake of the money but for the appreciation of City-men and the suburban halo which radiates from a bank balance typed in black. They think more of clean shirts and polished shoes than of clear heads and a polished style. They do not think of themselves as sovereign artists who give or are supposed to give intellectual valour to the community but behave as good and decent boys and hope to be rewarded by a knighthood at the end of their careers. English writers accept, and aim at, the standards of Victorian insurance brokers and county squires: it is financial success that counts, because good men please God and God rewards good men with cash.

Show me your bank account, the British public says, and it will define your place in our literature. Anyone with over £2,000 a year may rest assured of a place on our utility Olympus. Above that—Bow, bow, ye lower middle classes ! —we even give you a place in our gossip columns between paragraphs about a hunting earl and the night-club exploits of some minor royalty.

The main trouble is that the English public do not appreciate their writers as writers, but only as income tax payers and that most English writers agree with the public. In France (and in most other countries, even behind the Iron Curtain) a writer is somebody; in England he is nobody.

On the Continent—and I believe this definition touches the gist of the matter—a writer has some news-value, in England he has not. In this country if a film or stage actor, a minor radio-comedian or the half-back of a football team (second division) gets married, has a baby or is fined for having driven his car under the influence of drink, he will hit the headlines. The poor writer's marriage or baby pass unmentioned and he has at least to run someone over or beat up a policeman to be noticed. On the Continent a writer ranks equal—well, not with a first class boxer or a really glamorous music-hall singer—but certainly with a third rate actor. On the Continent a writer's company is coveted because he is a writer and not because he may be the member of a certain club or perhaps the second cousin of some nonentity with a title.

Now, would similar treatment make us happy ? Are we not sensible and mature persons, high above the hullaballoo of the vulgar mob ? No, we are not. Are we not happy that the gossip columns take no notice of us ? No, we are not. Do we wish to be treated by the gossip columnists as if we were the young and unmarried daughters of industrial barons just coming out ? Yes, we do.

This is, I hasten to add, a somewhat complex question. We do not desire these things for their own sake. Of course, we would not like to figure in the gossip columns and be photographed when getting married and coupled with silly society beauties. But we reserve the right to complain about such treatment; to feel indignant and outraged about it. But how can I complain about the vulgar press causing me endless trouble when the vulgar press takes no notice of me ? How can I complain about being pestered by photographers in my private life when photographers are not in the least interested even in my public life ? How can I haughtily refuse the invitation of the new rich and the new poor (the latter being the aristocracy) if they do not invite me ?

Many intellectuals, high-brows and writers would tell me that they entirely and totally reject the assessment of authors on an income-tax basis. They do not look up to a writer because he makes a lot of money, on the contrary, they look down upon best sellers and money-makers. This is as much as admitting that they, too, accept or reject a writer on purely financial grounds. Compare the person who says: " I am superstitious and never start any enterprise on the 13th," and the other person who laughs at him and says: " I am so completely lacking in all superstitious feelings that I start all my enterprises only and exclusively on the 13th." This second kind of person is the literary high-brow who condemns a book because it makes money and believes that his judgment is uninfluenced by financial considerations. Many people accept this attitude and are ashamed of their own successes. They blush in the presence of their colleagues who have succeeded in remaining failures. As if anybody has ever written a book with a view to its selling as badly as possible ! To sell well seems to be a blow to one's prestige; but somehow one can bear it.

ON A CRUSADE

I LIKE crusading.

Nowadays, however, it is a little difficult to decide on an object for one's crusade. This is a source of general embarrassment for English writers. The great periods of iterature are always the crusading periods but our age cannot quite make up its mind about its crusaders. Not that everything is so rosy in our time; but everything is so confused.

Let us throw a quick glance at the possibilities. The crusader needs, first of all, an idea and a slogan; some grand inspiring aim. A man of progressive ideas draws his sword and looks around. There are no unemployed anywhere and no hunger marches. The only unemployed is the poor crusader himself. (I am talking now of Britain and of British writers.) You can, of course, aim at the abolition of the shilling charge on national health prescriptions or the improvement of the dental service. But neither of these aims can really fill you with enthusiasm. In the twenties, you could write a soul-shattering novel or a revolutionary play about a family who lived on the dole and starved; but you cannot write a soul-shattering novel or a revolutionary play about a family whose dental treatment is good but could be better and who have to pay a shilling when buying bicarbonate of soda. A martyr who fought and died for jobs and security for all workers was a hero; a martyr—probably no less a man—who fights and dies for the false teeth of Britain seems a much less romantic figure.

If the modern writer tries to approach the matter from a more conservative angle, he is not much better off either. He may weep over the indignities befalling the rich and the decline of the middle classes. But a lament is not a crusade. Sobbing and shedding tears may be justified—but what is to be his slogan and his marching song? He cannot send his hero to the barricades and make him shout: " Down with the

Banner with a strange device

Sur-tax !" He cannot describe a man hit by a bullet, bleeding
to death on the pavement and whispering his last words to a
comrade: " Unearned incomes should be tax free !"

Nationalism is also out of date in these islands, even
Scottish and Welsh nationalism is confined within certain,
almost reasonable limits.   Dreams of wider loyalties are
utopian.   No-one could write a convincing scene in a novel
in which the hero leads a crowd of demonstrators frantic with
enthusiasm about North Atlantic unity.   Then, there is
Communism, but if you become a Stalinist, you have to
betray all Communist ideals and if you remain true and faithful
to Communist doctrines, then the Communists will rank
among your most determined enemies. This is where confusion
begins—but not where it ends.   If you are a sincere Socialist
you have to embrace America and turn against the Soviet
Union; if you are a rabid Tory you have to outbid the
Socialists in many fields; if you are a true Pacifist, you must
oppose the Peace Campaign; if you are a true Democrat, you
must ally yourself with Fascist Spain.   And so on.   A tough
time for crusaders.

Shortage in crusading material is as disconcerting for a
writer as shortage of fish is for a housewife.   Of course, the
crusader is not always drawn towards the noblest aims.   Few
of the original crusaders cared about the redemption of the
Holy Sepulchre.   They were driven by love of adventure;
hope of loot; by creditors; by a bank-manager who was
awkward about over-drafts; or even because the Crusade was
a good excuse for leaving a nagging wife, who was growing old
and unattractive.   Or for scores of other reasons—none of
which had much to do with the ostensible aim of the crusade.
But they all felt quite certain that they were noble crusaders,
doing their sacred duty to God and Church.   Similarly, the
crusading writer is not always a hero single-minded in his
intention: to speak the truth as he sees it.   He may utter his
unorthodox or shocking doctrines just *pour épater le bourgois*
—just to shock people; or to draw public attention to himself ;
or because he loves a good row; or because a good row is often

extremely profitable; or because he loved posing to himself as a crusader.

I know this today. I did not know it a few years ago when I set out on my own private crusade which resembled the original ones in at least one important aspect; it took me to the Holy Land.

When I decided to write a book on the new State of Israel, a little crisis broke out. My publisher asked me whether it was my intention to write a humorous book on the Jews. I told him that I did not know. It all depended, I said, on what I should see there. " If I find these people funny," I said, " I shall write a humorous book; if I find them tragic heroes of a Jewish Valhalla, I'll write a tragic book and everybody will weep over it." My publisher was not satisfied with this answer and firmly declared that I was not to touch the subject. Wounds were still open (this was in the spring of 1949); the British were still sore about recent events; Israel was too young a nation to be treated in a funny way. There were certain subjects—he went on—that one did not joke about. Such a book would offend all and please none. These were the strong views of my publisher and it was obvious that I needed reinforcement. I brought many of my friends into the battle and they—one after the other—took the publisher's side. Then I called in some neutral literary arbitrators who likewise all sided with my publisher and my friends. Finally I called in my wife who was also outraged and declared that this time I was really going too far. Having settled everything so neatly, I travelled to Israel and wrote a book about that fascinating country.

The book, when it appeared in 1950, was well received. But instead of feeling triumphant, I felt disappointed; instead of saying to my former opponents: " I told you so," I was mortified. It was some time before I could account for these feelings. Looking for an explanation, I arrived at a simple glorification of my motives. It was this: I had no idea that the book would be well received but the truth was that I did not care. I thought that so long as I was fair and said

what I really felt and thought and saw, it did not matter
how people received my report. This was an imaginary
pose. We all see ourselves like this. We are the men who
speak our minds fearlessly; who sacrifice success and
popularity for the love of truth; and so on. The simple fact
was that I had been engaged—without being aware of it—in
one of my crusades. In the crusade of a pugnacious adventurer
—not of a humble and fearless knight. I had pictured myself
in a heroic pose fighting with the English, Jews, Arabs,
friends and foes, publishers, critics and readers single-handed.
It took me a long time to grasp the situation. There was one
British periodical—a right wing journal—which was kind to
me in the way I had expected: it attacked me for having
touched the subject at all. All the other English papers were
kind in the more accepted sense of the word. The Zionist
press of London was most generous and the *Jerusalem Post*
wrote a leading article on my book. One can usually rely,
at least, on a few rude letters from readers. But even they
disappointed me bitterly. I received many letters from
different parts of the world—all pointing out a few mistakes I
had made in spelling some Hebrew words, but all telling me
how good-natured my book was. My last hopes were the
Arabs. I really thought that I had treated them harshly
and I considered it their patriotic duty to rise in protest.
The Middle East, however, remained fairly calm for a time
and I could not persuade myself that trouble brewing shortly
afterwards in Egypt had much to do with my book. No, the
Arabs let me down in an unpardonable way and the crowning
insult was that a short while ago an Arab diplomat very
kindly invited me to go to his country to write a book about it.

This was a tragedy—the tragedy of a crusader. If the
crusader is attacked, abused, torn to pieces, gibed at and
lampooned, he may feel happy. He has achieved his aim.
If he is engaged in a fight and is wounded—well, that is an
honourable fate for any fighter. Even being burnt at the
stake has its point. But what can be more unbalancing and
disturbing for the poor crusader—in full armour, complete

with helmet, shield and spear—than to be patted on the back by friend and foe alike ?   A bolt from the blue is bad enough ; a blessing from the blue can be almost as bad.

PART II. *Sociological*

MY IVORY TOWER

YOU enter the lift and push the button. Then you get out and walk up four floors because the lift is out of order. Outside my flat you push another button and nothing happens because the apparatus is out of order. Even if it were not, it would not ring because it is not a bell. It is an electric switch, disguised as a bell. Its original function was to light up the staircase for three minutes whenever pushed. But it does not light up the staircase for three minutes because it is out of order. Many of my visitors push that electric switch, wait for a few minutes, push it again and then go home. It is quite a good arrangement, and has functioned to my greatest satisfaction for ten years.

Those who know the trick and knock on the door may enter what—for lack of any suitable word in the English language—must be described as my flat. Judging by the rent I pay, it is a modern flat. Everything is there which modern ingenuity can offer you in discomfort, lack of space and silliness of design. It is lavishly furnished in the best Georgian style. (I mean George VI style, also called utility.)

People usually enter through the South Door because that is the only one. They find themselves in a corridor. The main piece of furniture there is a coat-hanger bought by my father-in-law at an auction for 7/6. It was not a bargain; I am always afraid that it will collapse under the weight of the heavier kind of rain coat. There are also two short carpets in the corridor, bought by my father-in-law at an auction. I do not remember the price but they were not bargains.

If you proceed from the South Door in a northerly direction, you find the East Wing on your right and the West Wing on your left. The first door on the right is Judy's room. Judy is my three year old daughter. Her room was nicely redecorated a short while ago and her room is quite all right except for the fact that it is shaped like a snake, or a cigar. Judy has a bed, two small pink cupboards, a small pink table with two small pink armchairs and a big basket where she refuses to keep her toys and books. The walls of the room are decorated with figures from the collected works of Walt Disney.

Room No. 2 in the East Wing is my room, generally called Daddy's room or George's room. When my little son stays with us he sleeps in this room, so it is also called Martin's room. Every now and then it is referred to as the guest room and sometimes again as the dining room. Nobody has ever called it the study and, I must say, that name would sound a little bombastic. I have two bookshelves, one by the West and one by the South wall, and Judy keeps her various belongings behind the rows of my books. The other day I found behind the books on the West shelf two wooden spoons, the handle of an old umbrella, the manuscript of a humorous novel sent to me by a Jamaican lady, one sock, a doll's head, a Teddy-bear's left leg, a pair of plastic knickers and three thousand Greek drachmai. A few months ago, I had two original drawings of some value framed. When I brought them home I put them up on top of the West bookshelf. Judy gave the bookshelf a push and one of the drawings fell down between the shelf and the wall. Whereupon Martin very politely jumped up to get it out for me. So he gave the shelf another push and the second drawing, too, fell down between the shelf and the wall. The drawings have been there ever since. By the North wall stands a large armchair which can be opened up and used as a fairly comfortable bed. In Hungary, they used to advertise these pieces of furniture by the slogan: "a chair by day, a bed by night." Frederic Karinthy once complained that he must have bought a faulty specimen because his was a bed by day and a chair by night, and consequently quite useless. Mine is faultless in this respect but Martin made a big hole in the material—in the most conspicuous place—and my wife and myself declare at least once a fortnight that the hole must be seen to, perhaps even mended. At the easternmost point of the room, under the window, standy my writing desk. It is a beautiful piece, a birthday present from my wife. On the desk itself, I keep cigarettes, unanswered letters, about three dozen reference books, a lamp, the telephone, two boxes full of pencils, four bottles of ink, a large ashtray and a wedding-day photograph of my wife and myself. The drawers of my desk used to have knobs—a couple of knobs each—by means of which you could pull them in the good old days. Judy's favourite pastime is pulling these knobs off the drawers. I am pleased to say that she has been successful with fourteen knobs, leaving me two knobs altogether—unfortunately both on the same drawer. The drawers—with the exception of one—cannot be opened now, except by using various tricks and devices such as tilting the desk and kicking its back side. The drawers, as well as some large boxes placed on the floor, contain my various manuscripts which I wished to save for posterity. I am afraid posterity has suffered an irreparable loss because Judy loves tearing out the pages of my manuscripts in order to draw on the backs. As this activity keeps her fairly quiet and as I am more concerned with my own present than with humanity's future, I let her do it. Many of my contracts, letters received and copies of letters sent have gone the same way: but I do not really believe in keeping documents. Nor does Judy.

Under my window lies Lord Cricket Ground where 35,000 people start clapping, cheering and yelling on the slightest provocation, during those periods of the year which the English—with charming irony—call spring and summer. Around me, a dozen radios howl all day but as I received my early training in an editorial office and am rather placid by nature, all this does not disturb me in the least. 35,000 yelling cricket enthusiasts, a dozen roaring radios, the sound of my manuscripts being torn up and a peacefully drawing child just fail to make any impression on me.

The rest of the flat—the sitting room which is the third room in the East Wing, the bed-room in the North Wing and the kitchen and bathroom in the West Wing belong to my wife's sphere of authority so they are in a more civilised state. It is true that the flat—with the exception of Judy's room—has not been redecorated from time immemorial because I keep declaring I shall buy a house, but as my wife has not yet succeeded in persuading me to go and see an agent, she has now decided that the flat should be redecorated—whether I buy a house or not. I must mention a three piece suite (two armchairs and a settee) in the sitting room which my wife bought at an auction and which was the object of bitter litigation for three years. An agent claimed commission on them and sued me. I love law-suits, indeed I have a passion for them, so I defended the case with vigour and with all my powers of rhetoric. All my friends were invited to the hearings to St. Marylebone County Court and I always had a nice audience. I won my case, with 7/6 costs. Then the agent sued my wife under her maiden name and we won the case again with another 7/6 costs. Finally, he sued us jointly and in the end I had to pay him about four pounds. The three piece suite may not be a collector's delight; it may not be a source of exhilarating aesthetic beauty; but it certainly was the source of endless amusement for me. As pieces of furniture they are matters of taste; as pieces of entertainment they were superb.

Should I become bankrupt and destitute I have an excellent idea. I shall imitate the example of many other great families of the land and I shall open the East Wing of my flat to the public. Goodwood House, no doubt, is larger, but my flat is more decayed. It is not exactly Tudor but it is a pretty ruin all the same. The sights should be excellent value for sixpence and the English are always ready to come and admire anything so long as they can queue up. I shall allow everybody to sign the Distinguished Visitors Book for a mere threepence extra.

Stately home

THE ARTIST AS COOK

I FEEL it my duty to give some short but valuable advice to young writers. Before you set out on the path of professional writing, you must remember that writing is an easy profession. Everybody can write; even among professional writers the percentage of those who can write is as high as 12.37. Everybody can write but only a few people can read and that makes the job a shade more difficult. A writer does not undertake any heavy responsibilities as is so often stated—nor does he play an important part in creating public opinion; in most cases it is public opinion which plays an important part in creating the writer's views. Writing is a nice, quiet occupation, especially for Englishmen who like privacy. Nobody knows what the writer is doing and nobody cares.

Professional writing has only one great drawback. You have to write. Look at those long novels, in ponderous volumes. They all had to be written from the beginning to the end, word by word. All that takes time and the modern writer has no time to write. On the following pages I shall summarise the writer's everyday duties and give a few hints to beginners on how to execute them in the best and most economical way.

GENERAL HOUSEHOLD DUTIES (HOW TO GET OUT OF THEM). Your wife will explain to you that as she is looking after the baby except (1) when she is not, and (2) when you are looking after it, it is only fair that you should (a) make the breakfast, (b) clean the flat, (c) do the shopping, (d) do the cooking, (e) lay the table, (f) do the washing-up, (g) do the drying up, (h) wash nappies, (i) sing to the baby for half an hour until it falls asleep, (k) tell stories to the bigger children before they go to sleep, (l) prepare supper and return to pionts (d), (e), (f) and (g) again.

I advise all young writers to accept these duties in principle without a murmur—indeed, with enthusiasm—and then get out of them gradually, as best they can. If you do not undertake these duties, your wife will be bound to observe that while she is working hard in the kitchen, you just sit in front of your desk looking in the air. She will naturally and reasonably suggest that you should do the cooking and the drying, and stare in the air at the same time thus killing two birds with one stone, as it were.

My own technique in getting out of these duties was: (a) boundless enthusiasm for all house-work; (b) doing jobs with frantic devotion but very badly; (c) dropping and breaking whatever I laid hands on; (d) constant admiration for my wife's prowess, dumbfounded astonishment at her ability coupled with challenging remarks to egg her on; (e) subtle and indirect stories about unrivalled excellence of domestic helps in this country. The result is that by now I have much less to do than is really fair and yet, I have the feeling that I have fooled only myself. I feel terribly uncomfortable; I have a bad conscience. Instead of being a martyr myself I have allowed my wife to become one and all my feeble efforts to make amends are turned down with an angelic smile. Where are the happy days when I could leave off my tiresone, boring writing whenever I wanted to, on the plea that I had to peel potatoes or do the washing up ? Instead of pleasant and romantic culinary exercises, I must stick to the dull slavery of writing. Young writers would be wise to ruminate over my far too successful exploits. There is nothing so melancholy in life as complete success; nothing more disconcerting than the perfect fulfilment of a dream.

COOKING. Even so, however, I have kept to myself certain duties which I regard more as prerogatives than as obligations. One of them is cooking. I do not think there is any living writer—including all dramatists and poets—who is a better cook than I am. I hate boasting but in this case I must blow my own trumpet. If Shakespeare could taste my

Pale with envy

goulash he would turn pale with envy; if Mr. T. S. Eliot were to try my *Hamburger à la Richelieu* (I cook almost everything *à la Richelieu*, it comes naturally to me) he would learn true humility. Once I cooked a Transylvanian *Fatányéros* for the late André Gide. He became more and more contemplative as he was consuming it. Swallowing the last bit, he stood up, picked up the manuscript of his latest novel which was lying nearby, turned to me and said: " Compared with you, Mikes, I am a sheer beginner." And he threw the manuscript into the fire.

Some cooks are born, others are made. I was made. Before leaving Hungary, I went to say goodbye to the editor of a theatrical weekly, who gave me a cookery book as a present.

" I don't know how to cook and I don't intend to learn," I said to him cheerfully, after I had thanked him.

" Every man has to cook in England," he replied. He knew England well but I did not take him seriously. But as he also gave me a generous parting gift in the shape of ready money, I thought I might as well please him by accepting the cookery book too. Unpacking my suitcase in London I found the book. I glanced at it, flung it back in the case and forgot all about it.

A few months later—this was still before the outbreak of the war—I took a furnished flat with two friends of mine: the actor whom I have mentioned earlier and a theatrical producer who too had been a member of the Hungarian National Theatre. We discovered with delight that we had a kitchen in the flat. It occurred to us that we might use it But who could cook ?

" I,"—I volunteered modestly.

" Good," exclaimed the two others. " Are you a good cook ?"

" Excellent. But my répertoire is somewhat limited."

" What can you cook ?"

" Scrambled eggs," I replied.

" Nothing else ?"

" Nothing else. But what's the matter with scrambled eggs ?"

There was nothing the matter with scrambled eggs. We all liked it and I cooked it with brilliant skill. We had scrambled eggs for breakfast, scrambled eggs for lunch and scrambled eggs for dinner, followed—at breakfast time preceded—by tinned pineapple which we all loved. We stuck to this diet except when we went out for a meal and felt happy and content with it. After five weeks we all started itching. We had no idea what was wrong with us until a doctor friend cross-examined us on our diet and told us that we needed more Vitamin A or B or C or D—I forget which.

" Very well," my producer friend declared, "we are going to cook proper meals."

" But how ?"

They turned to me:

" You are sure you cannot cook anything else but scarmbled eegs ?"

" Positive."

" Not even fried eggs ?"

" No."

" Then I shall do the cooking !" declared the producer grimly.

I suddenly remembered my cookery book and produced it from the bottom of my suitcase. My producer friend told us that he would cook *goulash*. He sounded rather as Napoleon Bonaparte must have sounded 150 years earlier when he declared he would invade England. The producer looked up the chapter on "*Goulash*" and declared:

" Not bad. Not bad at all. But I am going to improve on it."

We begged him not to improve on it but he insisted. And he did improve on it. He had never tried to cook before but, as it turned out, he had not only a knack, but real genius for it. The actor and I went on messages for him, did the shopping and ran back for various ingredients he had forgotten. He created new dishes; modernised old ones; perfected traditional food. In three weeks, our *cuisine* was famous in our circle. Our English friends loved it and the Hungarians loved it even more. My friend the producer was the creative genius but I had the imitative instinct. He created; I only cooked. He prepared dishes with his heart; I only with my brain remembering precisely what he had done. And I was not doing badly either.

I had, however, one great handicap. I was terrified of boiling fat. This meant I could not go near a frying pan. So I developed spectacular skill in throwing chipped potatoes from one end of the kitchen into the frying pan. My aim was uncanny. I never missed a throw-in but the walls soon became so festooned that I had to curb myself. Henceforward we ate mashed potatoes all the time.

I am still an acceptable cook, indeed a cook above the average: this is my one asset which makes me a desirable husband. I still love cooking. Youthful enthusiasm has by now been replaced by the sober methods of a more mature artist. My wife does not cook—she started working in an office very young and never had an poportunity of learning. Whenever she makes an attempt to learn, I discourage her. It is my sphere of authority; my contribution to the household duties; my only chance of leaving my desk for the sake of creative work.

As a cook, all the same, I am a hack. No young writer should write in the way I cook. My cooking—popular among my friends—is the "best seller" kind of cooking. I take ready made ingredients and mix them together according to well known recipes. There is no wit or originality in my cooking. I follow the popular taste and as my dishes have an exotic, Hungarian touch, people are prepared to take this for originality. My *goulash* (to take one example, although I could mention any of my dishes) is a type, not an individual; it has spice but lacks thought and deeper emotion; its technical brilliance and the cleverness of the construction cannot make up for a certain lack of inner conviction. It has touches of humour but lacks real fire. You can spend an agreeable quarter of an hour over my *goulash*, but it has really nothing new to say to the world.

SHOPPING. The other household activity I like is shopping. I do not shine at it. Indeed, I have proved a complete failure at shopping and my wife has now prohibited me from pursuing this favourite hobby of mine, except in cases of emergency. But in earlier years I enjoyed myself endlessly. Few people got as much out of queueing at the butcher's as I did. I was fascinated by the people I met and I always had excellent company: every morning, I met a painter and a barrister friend of mine with whom I discussed the international situation and exchanged market views.

My favourite greengrocer was an Italian called Mrs. Riccioni. I frequented her shop because I found her extremely picturesque. She was a bit of Italian folklore in St. John's Wood—and what more can one expect from one's greengrocer? She charged double price for everything but I never noticed it. Mrs. Riccioni—a very fat lady of 70—was a grand woman in her way. She spoke perfect cockney without a trace of a foreign accent. During the war she told me once: " I came to this country 50 years ago. I have 13 children, 9 of them in the army—and still I am a blooming foreigner here."

She ruled over her tiny meek little husband, and innumerable children, grandchildren and great-grandchildren with a rod of iron. She was the hardest worker of them all, she opened before 8 in the morning and stayed open till 9 in the evening, including Sundays. She charged preposterous prices but her faithful customers could get everything they wanted—and very good quality of everything with only a certain amount of rotten stuff thrown in. Among her many customers there was a little old Italian widow—who baffled me for a long time. This lady was something of a riddle for me as she was the only one who dared to bargain with Mrs. Riccioni. And when I say bargain, I mean it in the Italian, indeed the Southern Italian, sense of the word. It went like this: Signora P. picked up a cabbage and asked its price in English. "Eightpence," said Mrs. Riccioni, casually turning back to another customer. "No, I mean *this* cabbage." Signora P. repeated her question as if it had been an obvious misunderstanding. "Yes, that one. Eightpence," Mrs. Riccioni declared again in a rather more bellicose tone. A short pause, then Signora P.: "Threepence." This was meant to be an offer. Hoarse laughter from Mrs. Riccioni. "I've paid sixpence for it myself. The devil take me right away if I paid a farthing less. It's a beautiful cabbage." "This?" Signora P. laughed sarcastically. "Do you mean this? Its heart is soft and the leaves are rotten. I only wanted to buy it to save you the trouble of throwing it away. But I shan't give more than threepence halfpenny for it." "Sevenpence," Mrs. Riccioni replied sternly, implying that this was her last word in the matter. Signora P. threw the cabbage down and walked away with an ironical smile on her lips. She returned half an hour later and the battle of the cabbage continued. The more Mrs. Riccioni praised and extolled the cabbage, the more Signora P. made desparaging and derogatory remarks about it. Signora P. broke off negotiations about three times. Then the parties changed their language and burst out in vociferous and uproarious Italian, accusing each other of cheating, black marketeering and stinginess. In the end Signora P. carried away the cabbage in triumph—for fivepence halfpenny.

I always enjoyed their skirmishes and their major engagements but never understood either of them. I knew that Signora P. was reasonably well off and I also knew that she would never dream of bargaining in any other shop. Mrs. Riccioni again had hundreds of agreeable and easy customers, why on earth did she waste her time on Signora P.? It took me more than a year to grasp the situation. Signora P. was the only customer for whom Mrs. Riccioni had any respect. She felt deep contempt for all her sheeplike English customers (and myself) who paid her atrocious prices. She looked down on us all and regarded us as miserable fools whom even she, a simple and illiterate Italian peasant woman, could cheat

And she felt cheated herself. They were paying any price she asked for; so she felt she should have asked more. Signora P. was different. She was intelligent; she knew how to look after her money; she was a real lady; she was a bit of Italy. Only Signora P. and Mrs. Riccioni knew that shopping was a battle of wits. The others did not really count.

Yes, shopping in Italy is an intellectual pastime, better than reading but not quite as good as the pictures. There are no prices in Italy in the English sense of the word: the price of a commodity is what the skill and perseverance of the customer can make it. You can bargain for theatre tickets, and even successful bargaining for postage stmaps is not unheard of.

Shopping in England is a different kettle of fish altogether. It is a great national pastime but not an intellectual, only a social, activity. The English, to their great credit, are no intellectuals. Millions of women (and quite a few men) are on the move all day long doing local shopping or West End shopping. Local shopping is hard work but most enjoyable because it is bound up with such delightful activities as walking in the rain and queueing. West End shopping is a purely social and not a mercantile activity. Before the war, a friend of mine knew a girl, a married woman, who spent all her weekday afternoons with my friend. At 6 o'clock she had to hurry home to meet her husband. I often met her and got to know her quite well. Once, I asked her how she could get away every single afternoon in the week. " I tell Reginald that I'm going shopping," she explained. " Every afternoon ?" I asked. " Yes, every afternoon." " And doesn't your husband find it peculiar that you never buy anything ?" She looked at me wide-eyed. " Oh no—of course not." Her voice betrayed a great deal of irritated astonishment. What an idiotic question ! What has shopping got to do with buying things ?

I am not doing much shopping nowadays. I am not allowed to set foot in Mrs. Riccioni's establishment since my wife discovered that she is a robber. In vain do I come forward with my theories that Mrs. Riccioni is only a master-bargainer, my wife is unimpressed. Mrs. Riccioni has different views on shopping and prices from my wife; it is the clash of two *Weltanschaunngen*; they will never understand each other. In the meantime, I must not enter her shop, nor am I allowed to do any West End shopping. My wife knows my technique too well. I always buy the first pair of shoes shown to me, whatever its size, and the first overcoat, whatever its colour. So shopping plays only a minor part in my life but other household duties, especially cooking, still rank high. Whenever I have a little time left free, I do some writing.

I remember a vulgar but characteristic little story which I heard in Vienna, where public conveniences are few and far between. A man made several attempts on various street corners but the police always interfered and chased him away. In despair, the man walked up to a doctor whose brass plate caught his eye and complained that he was unable to carry out certain natural and normal activities. Two minutes later the doctor was completely taken aback as he watched his phenominal performance. "Why did you say that you couldn't?" the doctor asked angrily. "Oh I can," the patient replied, "but only if they give me a chance."

This explains the plight of many authors of our age. Yes, we can write, but only if they give us a chance.

THE ARTIST AS MERCHANT

THERE are two main lines of argument which writers use to reassure themselves if they feel any doubt about their own excellence. The first: " I am a popular author, enjoyed by the wide reading public; consequently I must be a brilliant artist." The other: " I am an unpopular author, rejected by the vulgar mob; consequently I must be a brilliant artist." If your position changes, change your argument, never forgetting—but never admitting—that the wide reading public is identical with the vulgar masses. There are stock examples and stock arguments to prove that you must be this or that in order to be a great man. You must be unsuccessful during your lifetime like Stendhal; you must be successful like Arnold Bennett. You must achieve success early like Maugham; or late like Pirandello. You must be born high and wealthy like Tolstoy; you must be born low and be a self-made man like Wells. You must write very little like E. M. Forster; or very much like Balzac. You must be a misanthropist like Flaubert: or a good mixer like Dickens. Of course, no-one has ever followed an example or recipe; one only picks out examples to prove—what ? Usually nothing at all. Not every rich, half-mad aristocrat is a Tolstoy, and not every man over sixty who takes up writing becomes a Pirandello. There may have been great writers who never washed their ears but it does not follow that one has only to abstain from washing one's ears to become a great writer.

I should like to be a popular author. If I am not one, it is not for want of trying. I do not say that I always compromise on matters of opinion and taste to please people or avoid rows. Not always but very often—just like everybody else. We all eschew certain subjects and leave certain things about which we feel strongly unsaid because we are afraid to say them. Often we are unwilling to make a stand and fight on questions which are important to the point of

284

our main argument. And often we are fooling ourselves. We are cowards posing as heroes. I, at least, am a coward posing as a coward.

Yes, I should like to be a popular writer. I am writing—amazing as it sounds—to be read and I wish people would read me more. I do not shun the vulgar masses; I run after them. I do not hate them; I am one of them. "Vulgar masses" is only an expression for the people who do not read or appreciate you (if you are a writer) or whose taste is different from yours (if you are a reader). There are people who are black and others who are white; some are poor, others are rich; some are English, others are foreigners; some had a good education, others educate themselves as well as they can; some are the children of country vicars, others of metropolitan burglars. I do not remember who it was who, about a hundred years ago, seeing criminals being led to the gallows, exclaimed: "There but for the grace of God go I." Whoever he was, he was a wise man. I know no vulgar cockneys nor vulgar dukes, nor tramps, nor scholars. If I meet any repulsive individual, I exclaim: "There but for the grace of God go I." No, I know no vulgar masses. As a man I know other men; as a writer I know readers. And I prefer many readers to few readers. It is not only their quality I am after; it is also their quantity. I do not write for the intelligent few; I write for the intelligent many. I am grateful for every sign of appreciation. I love getting letters from readers because these letters remind me of the fact that I am alive. One is not always certain. I have managed up to now to answer all the letters I have received, whether they come from East London or South Chile, whether they came from a shoemaker I knew in 1938 or Professor Einstein whom—unfortunately for me—I do not know at all. I have spent a lot of money and time on these letters; I wish I could spend more.

I am always delighted if anyone asks me to autograph a book. I am surprised that he should value my signature and—in many cases—disregard trouble and expense (usually my expense).

I am always deeply touched when I receive manuscripts from young authors. I especially like those who explain in an accompanying letter that the book has been written in my own stryle. I was never aware of having a special style; but if I have, I do not like other people writing in it. There are so many good styles lying around—can't they pick one for themselves?

I love being asked to give a lecture. Once, I was asked to do so for a lady's society which has a very misleading name. For the lecture I selected a paper on some literary subject, prepared some time before. It had been received kindly by other audiences but fell completely flat there because the ladies had really not the faintest idea what I was talking about. I changed and simplified as much of it as I could as I was jogging along but the result was disastrous. When our suffering came to an end, a kind lady—they were all very kind and sweet and old—moving a vote of thanks, addressed me: "We were not really interested in the least in what you were saying. We only wanted to see what you looked like." I was a little taken aback by this frank admission but decided later that I would take it as a compliment. Not because it was really meant as a compliment; but, when in doubt, I take everything for a compliment and this rule does a great deal of good to my self-esteem.

I think it must have been certain clever publishers who spread the notion that it does not become a lyric poet to be a good business-man. They kept on repeating "An author is not a merchant" until writers believed them. By clever propaganda they made writers accept the theory that the world of arts and the world of business are worlds apart and that he who excels in one must fail in the other. It follows clearly that since good writers must be bad business-men, all bad business-men must be good writers. Many writers have acted upon this assumption. Today it is no more compulsory for a writer to starve in a garret and die of tuberculosis at twenty-eight, although this still makes a favourable impression and secures at least one feature article (photo inserted) in the popular dailies. But even today it is not *chic* for a writer to read a contract before signing it; to know what $12\frac{1}{2}\%$ of 12/6 really means; and to treat your publisher as if he were a business-man and not a poet.

This may be a little surprising, because today the picture has completely changed. Writers take a primary interest in the business side of their activities and are, as a rule, confronted by poetic publishers who dream of art and literature (and all secretly write lyric poetry). In business deals, most writers are still undiplomatic. Vulnerable because vain, they all have an unerring eye for the irrelevant; but they all fancy themselves as shrewd business-men. Publishers, on the other hand, resent being treated as ordinary business people; after all they deal in books and not in toothpaste or tinned vegetables (as though this, in itself, meant anything), and like to parade as professional patrons of art. I know one publisher whose favourite adjective applied to himself is "talented";— meaning that he is extremely talented in putting nice, golden lettering on the spine of a book and dazzlingly ingenious in printing the right number of copies. He is convinced that all his successes are due not to the good work of the authors concerned but to the little changes he has asked them to make in punctuation and the good dust jackets he has had designed. His authors visit him regularly and enquire after sales figures. He gives the information with an air of detachment and boredom; his pride in his achievements is purely literary and artistic and he pockets his large monthly cheques with a deep sigh.

Look at me. My main ambition, too, is to shine as a business-man. I should love to achieve glittering success as a stockbroker (working, of course, under a pen-name).

Unfortunately, it is still a far cry before I become a "talented business-man". I have concluded one single business deal in my life—apart from signing contracts with publishers—and the result was disastrous. The financial part of it was not the worst; the real trouble was that it gave my wife an excellent story against me which she used ruthlessly— until recently.

In 1949 I knew that I was going to get a new car before long, and when I left London for two months in the autumn, I put an advertisement in the Personal Column of *The Times*, offering my small and ancient Ford car for sale for £300. My wife told me in advance—a strong point in her later attacks—that it was silly to advertise such a car in *The Times*. If I had a Rolls or a Daimler—she said—that would be different; but my old Ford? Some three men—all in bowler hats—came to see my car, all spat on it in disgust and told me that I could count them out as buyers. Then I had to leave London and the car was still unsold. One day before my return my wife was rung up by the manufacturer's office and informed that my new car was ready for delivery. On my arrival home the selling of the old car became a pressing and urgent matter. I advertised again, this time in *The Evening Standard* (" no dealers please "), and offered my car in quite decent condition, and added my telephone number, for sale for £200. A dealer telephoned at 9.30 a.m.—hours before *The Evening Standard* appeared—and I made an appointment with him in my garage, round the corner. I had to dress in a hurry and go down to meet the man. My wife warned me: " Don't sell it to the first man unless he pays the full price." I smiled superciliously: " Trust me." I went down to the garage and sold the car in five minutes for £175.

That was bad enough. But worse was to come. Our telephone kept ringing the whole day long. Several hundred people enquired. When they were told by my wife that the car had been sold, my wife often had to describe to them what it looked like. She grew angrier and angrier after each call and painted more and more terrifying pictures. She told the callers that the rain was falling through the roof, that the back seat was falling to bits; in the last few hours she added that we had lost the spare wheel and one other wheel, and the car was running on three wheels only. The enquirers were not discouraged. " Well, what can you expect for that money ? It sounds a lovely little car. If it was bought by a dealer, can you give me his address, please. He might resell for

Count them out

£225." Late that afternoon 'phone calls came from Birmingham and Wales and we received one telegram (reply prepaid) from Nonant-le-Pin, Orne, France. It was three full days before the storm calmed down completely (I mean the storm of telephone calls).

My wife was in despair, and forbade me henceforth to meddle in business. " You can cook," she said, "drive a car and write. But don't do any business." I was not quite happy about the order in which my wife listed my supposed accomplishments but remained silent. She added: " In future, I shall deal with business matters." And she did.

Our next business deal arose in connection with the slae of old newspapers—about three years after the car episode. A huge mountain of old newspapers had accumulated in our kitchen cupboard. When they started overflowing, I took large bunches to a nearby grocer. After a while, my wife protested. Why should one give away old newspapers ? One should sell them. (By the way, she is just as extravagant as I am, but every now and then she gets worked up about twopence-halfpenny.) I agreed. Her attitude suggested that *I* should sell them. I made it clear that I knew no gentlemen engaged in the waste-paper trade and had no idea how to get hold of one. "All right," she replied, " leave it to me," adding that, in any case, I would only make a mess of the whole affair and it would be such a pity to throw all this money out of the window. About a week later she came home with Judy one day about noon and I descried from her face and demeanour that momentous events were afoot. " My paper-merchant is calling in a few minutes." she told me as casually as she could. She added that she had met the head of a large firm who was calling from house to house with his own horse and cart and buying up all the waste paper in the district at phenomenal prices. I congratulated her warmly and returned to my room where I was writing something. A few minutes later, there was indeed a knock at the door. I heard my wife hand over a large bunch of paper to the man and then I heard him say:

" Have you got any more ?"

" Yes—heaps," my wife replied.

Then the man's voice after another thirty seconds:

" Is that all ?"

My wife: " Oh no—but you won't be able to carry any more."

The man: " Don't worry about me. Give me all your paper. I can carry the lot."

More paper was carried to the door and then I heard nothing else except the door being closed with a bang. No further conversation, no jingling of silver, no rustling of five pount notes.

When we sat down to lunch I asked my wife:

" That man who bought your papers . . . "

" Yes ?"

" Did he pay anything ?"

" No."

" Not a penny ?"

" No."

" Did he thank you for it ?"

" No."

" Did he say good-bye when he left ?"

" No."

We both thought of the selling of my car. My man, at least, paid *something* and shook my hand with noticeable warmth almost amounting to gratitude. My wife and I did not discuss the matter further. But since that day my wife has never made one critical remark about my business abilities.

And yet, I am absolutely certain that I have found the secret of making a real fortune. You must buy something very cheaply—very cheaply indeed—and sell it at a terrific price. I am now working on these lines but sticking to theories for the time being. I have already found things which can be bought very cheaply, but these would not sell at a high price; I have also discovered other goods which would fetch glittering prices but these again cannot be bought cheaply. There seems to be a snag in everything. But I am not discouraged. I feel I am about half way to success and I shall persevere.

MEMORIES FROM SIBERIA

I AM often astouded to find how ridiculously self-centred we all are. Meet a chartered auctioneer and estate agent for example: you'll find he hardly knows that there are other normal and even important activities in life apart from buying and selling houses. To professors and even students, " life " is synonymous with "university," and the rest of the world is only there to supply some background noises; while journalists firmly believe that the universe consists of Fleet Street and its neighbouring pubs and the rest of the world is only there to supply (a) raw material for news and (b) readers and advertisers. I used to be often surprised myself to find that not all the people around me were English humorists of Hungarian origin. But I have been taught to face facts and today I know better. Yet, I still retain one firm conviction of this nature which is never shaken by experience but is on the contrary confirmed every day. This is that "every boy and every girl that's born into the world alive" has been, is, or will be at one time in his or her career working for the BBC (also known as the British Broadcasting Corporation).

I firmly believe that humanity consists of three main groups: (1) BBC employees; (2) former BBC employees; (3) future BBC employees. The few people who do not belong to any of these groups are outside contributors of the BBC but their own group is hardly worth mentioning, being a *quantité négligeable*. Do not forget that the three groups described are not confined to writers, artists, actors, musicians and their like. Waitresses you have seen somewhere will turn up in BBC canteens; the electrician who mends your desk-lamp will turn up as a BBC electrician (or, true to BBC fashion, the waitress will turn up as an electrician and the electrician as a waitress, but that does not weaken my argument in the least). Once I got friendly with a grocer's assistant at Bracklesham Bay, near Chichester, where I was spending a summer; a few months later I met him as a liftman in one of the BBC buildings. A few months ago a lady-assistant in a tobacconist's told me she wanted to change her job and asked me whether I knew something for her.

" That depends," I replied. " What are your qualifications ? What can you do ?"

" Nothing," she said.

" Are you sure about that ?"

" Quite sure," she repeated firmly.

" If you are really not misleading me, I believe I can help you. The BBC always has a lot of vacancies for people like you."

I told her to whom to write and what to write and forgot all about our conversation. Six weeks later I met her in one of the BBC buildings. She greeted me with a grin and told me that she had been employed to deliver the internal post.

I am myself no exception to the general rule. I had better admit my failings. I am only human. I spent seven years on the staff of the Corporation. Before that, I was an outside contributor; now I am an outside contributor again—but until my dying day I cannot feel quite sure that I shall not become a BBC employee again. Indeed, as it has happened in the past that the BBC has issued service contracts, by mistake, to deceased individuals, even death does not mean absolute safety.

Still, I differ from the average human being in two respects. In the first place, I am not one of those millions who leave the BBC after many decades of service and then write a vitriolic attack upon it, describing the place in such a way that one can harldy understand how they stood it for more than five minutes. I am almost ashamed to confess it, but I quite liked my work and the Corporation. Secondly— this is the other important point of difference—I worked in Bush House, the headquarters of the European Service. Not in the "real BBC," as some people put it. If an engineer or editor is sent over from Broadcasting House to Bush House, he feels as if he had been sent to Siberia. On arrival, he is heart-broken and act as though his life were not worth living. Two months later he is a new man and—as a rule—would not return to the Home Service for love or money. Or to be more precise : not for love, only for money.

Contempt between B.H. (standing for Broadcasting House) and Bush House (which could also be abbreviated as B.H. but never is because it would be regarded as sacrilege) is mutual. I breathed the air of Bush House too long for me to change my mind now, but I believe that I am basing my views on matters of fact and predilection—not merely of old loyalty. I have always been and still am unable to listen to a broadcast in the Home Service or Light Programme (with some very few and, let us add, occasionally very notable exceptions). Their variety programmes, Twenty Questions, " I Beg to Differ "—kind of entertainment can chase me out of my home if my neighbours have their radio on too loud ; and I can enjoy poetry without Wilfred Pickles choosing it for me. My summary dismissal of these programmes may be a little unfair because many, indeed most, of them I have never heard from beginning to end. I simply did not have the nerve. There are famous comedians, celebrated throughout the land, whose very names I have never heard at all. I do not even buy *The Radio Times* because I simply do not care what is on. And—I know this sounds almost incredible—I was even able to control my emotions when Miss Gracie Fields married a gentleman by the name of Alparovici, described as a Bulgarian television expert. As there is no television in Bulgaria, I could not quite understand what the gentleman really was but I could resist the temptation to find out. (Maybe he has seen a television programme or two, and as very few Bulgarians have done so, he clearly ranks as an expert among them.)

The European Service—in which, I am glad to say, public interest is very moderate—at least tries to act on the premise that, through its medium, adults talk to adults, and very often it goes so far as to assume that intelligent adults talk to intelligent adults. As the audience consists only of foreigners, no objection is taken to this. The democratic

English masses, of course, would not stand for such treatment for a week.

On the *facade* of Bush House one reads: " TO THE FRIENDSHIP OF ENGLISH SPEAKING PEOPLES." In spite of this dedication, Bush House is one of the most cosmopolitan buildings in the world and English is spoken in most curious accents in its new canteen (which, by the way, looks like the operating theatre of a medium-sized hospital in Kansas, U.S.A.).

Walk around Bush House. In one studio the Germans may be rehearsing a Schiller drama, next door the Chinese are reading the news and in a third a jazz-programme is being broadcast to Finland. It is fascinating to see how the individual sections have kept their national characteristics— or more precisely to see what kind of mixture is the result of the reciprocal influence exercised by them on the English, and vice-versa. The Frensh Section reminds you of a madhouse. This is particularly true of French rehearsals in the studio. Everyone is excited, everybody is either joking or quarrelling with everybody else; nothing is really properly organised and even if it is, some key-man forgets the rules at the crucial moment and the rehearsal often ends in complete chaos. Not so the actual transmission. The main actor may decide to take off his shirt during one of his long and very dramatic soliloquies, but not a sinlge listener will notice that anything extraordinary is going on—and indeed, nothing extraordinary is going on. The result is almost always a brilliantly written, witty and informative programme, faultlessly delivered. The French do not get anglicised, on the contrary the gallicise the English who work with them. The English who live in this French island are either more French than the French, or else feel a little embarrassed and out of place, even after thirteen years.

The Germans are methodical and meticulous, living up to their reputation. No jokes in the studios. The studio is for them a temple, a serene and sacred shrine of boredom and flawless efficiency. They rehearse a whole week where others are content to rehearse a day. All their "impromptus" are prepared at least ten days before delivery, stamped and signed by higher officials, and all German announcers carry a huge log-book about with them; they finish reading with a keen eye on the studio clock and the moment they finish they fall on the log-book and start a little book-keeping exercise with frantic delight, jotting down exactly how many seconds before the minute they stopped reading, and a few dozen other small and equally thrilling details. When speaking to each other, they often use the formal " Sie" instead of the familiar " Du," even if they have been working together for ten years or so. Many of them have been living here for a long time and many behave in a heavy handed but quite natural way. They are highly cultured, absolutely reliable in all respects. As they cannot acquire charm they rather despise it.

Three Italians engaged in a friendly chat can make more noise than the average English mass-demonstration in Trafalgar Square. Any group of three Scandinavians can be so cool and aloof that the typical Englishman compared with them looks warm-hearted, emotional and jovial. The members of one European section (not of the North) are successful merchants of high renown and they import, let us say pineapples. Up to a few years ago they had plenty of free time for their commercial activities: then their bulletins increased rather inconveniently in number. So they sent a delegation to the management, asking for a reduction in the number of their buletins on the grounds that their official duties interfered with their hobbies and outside activities. The management would not oblige and this accounts for the pineapple shortage in Britain. When you meet the Poles in the corridor, they bow low with impeccable but formal and unsmiling courtesy. I always feel about the Poles that they are about the only people who are not just "doing a job" in Bush House to earn a living; they believe in their mission. They always seem to be thinking of those silent millions of peasants, far away in Eastern Europe, who have been cheated and fooled by almost all the peoples of Europe (including their own Polish lords and masters) throughout the centuries, but who never give up hope and who are always ready to fight everybody's battle, just to be cheated again. If I meet a Pole and he gives me a low bow and greets me with the politeness due from one ambassador to the other, I feel—being a member of the human race—that I owe him something. The Hungarians radiate a large amount of Central European charm which they switch on and off at will and they can get away with almost anything.

All these Continentals are anglicised to some extent, and the English of Bush House, having been exposed to reciprocal influences, have become continentalised in no small degree. In Bush House you will not meet with the poker faced stiffness of Broadcasting House. The English came to Bush House as colonisers and master but have become a tolerated minority. No Englishman there can really stand on his dignity as an Englishman. Some of them have become humanised; some of them almost capable of logical thinking; some have managed to become ill-mannered, even by Continental standards—a rare achievement on an Englishman's part—and some of them even learn Czech.

Many former BBC Employees, writing their vindictive memories, tell hair-raising stories of muddle and incompetence. Some of these tales are true. An organisation as vast as this— be it a broadcasting company, a motor car factory or a state— is bound to be bureaucratic, clumsy and often inefficient. Such defects are attendant upon size.

People finding fault with bureaucracy always pick on "filling up forms." This is silly. No modern organisation can be run without a large amount of clerical work and written documents, and most of these are necessary. Probably not all the copies of the forms, and not all the questions contained in them, are necessary, but that is a detail. The real disease of bureaucracy lies elsewhere. The true bureaucratic mind sees only cases, paragraphs, regulations and completely disregards, indeed, completely forgets that there may be some connection between his ugly files and real life.

He will never dare to spend twopence to save two thousand pounds if the twopence is likely to be queried by fussy auditors (i.e. other bureaucrats), whereas the expenditure of £2,000 is formally right. A few days ago I heard the following story. A girl who had rather a good job got married and wanted to emigrate to New Zealand with her husband. She gave notice to the Corporation expiring at the end of April, preparatory to leaving in May. Their departure, however, was postponed and she asked permission to stay on for another five months. Permission was first granted but later she was told that in view of the strict overall economy measures to be carried out throughout the Corporation, she would have to go when the original notice given by her expired. Naturally she understood and accepted this decision without a murmur.

A few days later, however, she was told that in order to compensate her for this disappointment she would receive a beneficial grant in one lump sum. This sum came to half as much again as her salary (which the Corporation could not afford to pay because of the new economy measures) would have been for the five months. They paid her £600 instead of £400, did without her services and probably employed another person for £400 to do her job. The net loss on this economy measure was £600. But on paper, somehow it looked like a saving and that was all that mattered. The bad kind of bureaucrat thinks not of the masses of listeners but only of his immediate superiors. It does not matter what millions of listeners feel so long as the whims or idiosyncracies of the man who writes his annual report are satisfied. Many administrators and executives are bound to overestimate their own importance, which is in most cases infinitesimal, and believe that commentators, announcers and script-writers are only there to give them some raw material to administrate. Indeed, all large organisations have a bureaucratizing effect on everybody in them, and only the best people (but quite few in number) succeed in remaining human, keeping their heads above the paragraphs and preserving a fairly sober judgment about their own importance.

The BBC is no exception to this general rule of large organisations. But the spirit of the Corporation is so fair and generous that few injustices really occur and if they occur they can always be remedied. There are quite a number of brilliant men in responsible positions, and as a rule the Corporation jealously guards the rights and interests of its staff. The Corporation is a fair employer; indeed, having come from Central Europe, I found it a fairer employer than I could ever have dreamt of. I learnt my way fairly quickly in the labyrinth of staff regulations—which are always exceedingly fair—and I could make a nuisance of myself whenever I decided to. I decided to do so fairly often because (a) certain bureaucratic pin-pricks annoyed me beyond reasonable measure, and (b) the game amused me. Still, I believe I can claim that I was just—though admittedly strict—to my immediate bosses.

The British are proud of their ability to create a muddle and then muddle through all difficulties. I must shake the British pride: muddle is not an exclusively British institution. Read descriptions, for instance, of the over-organised, wonderfully systematic and " thorough " German war-machine during the last war. But, let us admit, British muddle has its special flavour; it is unlike every other muddle in the world; it is unique, like the British character, with an isolationist touch in it. British and Imperial muddle never leads to violent scenes, never to base and groudless mutual accusations; it never costs its creators their heads. The basic difference between British muddle and foreign muddle is that the British are sensible enough to regard muddle as the natural and accepted state of things and to consider perfect order as a disquietening and natural phenomenon bound to end in disaster. British muddle is enchanting and peacefully winding like the Thames; it is like Soho: pleasant and most enjoyable, but you have no idea how you got in or how you are going to get out. British muddle is as national in character as the British constitution and, indeed, one logically follows from the other. The British kind of muddle is one of the few national treasures not for export. We are proud of it. And do not forget that, after all, the BBC is one of our great national institutions.

My connections with the BBC started with a conspiracy on their part to inveigle me into the German service. I told them quite openly at the outset that I spoke no German—which probably accounts for it.

Soon after the outbreak of the war I applied for a job in the Hungarian Section, but there was no vacancy. I was disappointed and thought that there the matter ended—at least until a vacancy occurred. But far from it.

Some time afterwards the Establishment Officer's secretary rang me up and asked me whether I knew German. I said I was extremely sorry but I knew no German. She sounded not only disappointed but annoyed by this answer. " I was told," she argued, " that all Hungarians talk German." " Who told you so ? " I asked politely but playfully. " A gentleman who should know," she said icily. " In that case I must be an exception. I know no German." A moment's silence followed, then the cross-examination continued " What language do you actually talk then ? " " Hungarian," I said. I felt that she was raising her eyebrows. " What ? Hungarian ? Do you mean to say that that is a separate language ? " she exclaimed and I knew that she disapproved of the fact. " Yes. It may be a small language; it may be unimportant but it is quite separate." Another brief interval while she collected her thoughts for the next wave of the attack. " Don't you know even a little German ? " She had me there. Now it was my turn to hesitate. " Yes," I whispered, " I know a little German." My defences had collapsed. Counsel had pinned me down to an important admission. She intructed me curtly to appear in a certain room in Broadcasting House at 11 a.m. next morning. She did not even tell me what for.

At the appointed time I was ushered into a large room where a wireless set was blaring martial music and seven or eight German ladies and gentlemen were sitting round the table. We were not introduced to each other. I sat down speechlessly while they eyed me and each other with some suspicion. I felt like telling them: " Ladies and gentlemen, please do not be anxious on my account." We were all given pencils and paper but nobody told us what to do with them. But it was obvious enough. Presently the martial uproar stopped, a German announcer identified the station as *Deutschlandsender* and began to read out the *Wehrmacht* communiqué and one more news item concerning the Russo-Finnish war. Both items were full of long names and the second even of interminable and unpronounceable Finnish place-names. The Germans around the table made swift squiggles with their pencils, and at the same time kept looking around and trying to express their general deportment that they had plenty of time to spare. I gave it up after thirty seconds and leaned back in my chair. I knew no shorthand—not even Hungarian. At last the announcer stopped and after a short pause made the surprising declaration: "And now I am going to repeat the news-bulletin at dictation speed." I pricked up my ears and picked up my pencil. I put down everything carefully and without the slightest effort. Whenever the announcer came to a proper name—German or Finnish—he spelt it out. My German fellow-competitors were now sitting around the table in various reclining attitudes or leaning back in their chairs, looking up in the air and occasionally throwing contemptuous and puzzled glances at me. I went on scribbling busily.

Next day, I was offered a job as German monitor. I had to decline it with thanks, explaining again, this time to some higher official, that (a) I did not know German properly and (b) I did not know shorthand in any language. (Today I know that I was foolish to refuse a good job. Nobody would even have noticed my slight deficiencies.)

The BBC, however, is a great and illustrious national institution and one slight setback did not divert it from its purpose. It had set its heart on turning me into a German monitor. And it made yet onather gallant attempt.

Scribbling busily

This was about three years later. By that time I had become a regular outside contributor to a number of sections and in this way made a livelihood—such as it was. One day the Establishment Officer (not the one I mentioned above) asked me to visit him. I did. I was taken into his room. Next to him, there was a silent, bespectacled gentleman at the table. He looked extremely uncomfortable. The Establishment Officer told me that I was making rather more money from my outside work than an ordinary member of the staff, so they thought they might offer me a job as a script writer. Would I accept it ? With pleasure, I replied. Very well, he continued, he was going into the Army next week but his successor—and he pointed to the grim gentleman, suffering at his table— would take the matter in hand. He did. A fortnight later I was called in to see him. He told me I was being given a job as German monitor at Evesham Worcestershire. Would I be ready to start next Monday ? No, I said, not next Monday or any other Monday morning this century. In the early 21st Century, I said, I would be prepared to reconsider the matter.

Once when Francis Joseph, Emperor of Austria and King of Hungary passed through a certain tiny Hungarian village before World War I, the bells failed to ring out. The King turned to the Mayor and asked him sternly: " Why aren't the bells being rung ?" The Mayor, a timid little man, terrified out of his wits, replied: " We have three reasons for this, Your Majesty. The first is that we have no bells. The second . . . " Francis Joseph interrupted him: " Well, you need not tell me the other two."

During the interview with the new Establishment Officer I was less lucky than the Mayor. He asked me why I did not want to accept a German monitor's job at Evesham. I had three reasons, I said. The first was that I knew no German. The second . . . and I waited for the interruption. But I had to tell him all my reasons and even when I had finished he started persuading me with the following skilful arguments. (1) I was making more money from the Coporation than I ought to. (2) His instructions were to start a thorough drive for German

monitors because really efficient German monitors were scarce.
(3) I showed some ability in writing, consequently he wanted
me to go to Evesham as a German monitor. Put in that way,
the argument, of course, sounded sane and forceful; but, I
did not go.

Towards the end of the war, when I had no longer any
wish to join the BBC, a vacancy occurred in the Hungarian
Section. I did not apply for the post. One day, when I was
chatting with a friend on the third floor in Bush House, a
gentleman passed to whom my friend spoke. This gentleman
turned out to be called the Manager of the Hungarian Section.
"Oh," said the Manager, "don't you want a job in the
Hungarian Section?" I was completely taken aback. "No,"
I replied. "Not really." Not a full hour after uttering
"not really," I became a member of the Hungarian Service.
I stayed in my job for almost seven years.

For seven years I went through the mill. And I liked it.
Bush House grows on you; it has an atmosphere; you feel that
you belong to it and it belongs to you; it has a magnetic
fascination. I keep cropping up in Bush House on visits,
long and short—often without any particular reason—and
cannot quite define the nature of my visits. Do I visit Bush
House as one visits a famous battlefield, the scene of ancient
glories? Or as the criminal returns to the scene of the crime?
I have done and written and seen much during my seven years
but there are only three feats of which I am really proud.

(1) I am a musical ignoramus. I cannot sing or whistle
in tune the simplest nursery rhyme. As far as I am concerned
Beethoven might never have written his symphonies. I prefer
Sullivan any day. Let us be outspoken: I am a musical
half-wit. Little wonder, then, that some years ago I was
chosen to serve the BBC as a music critic. Of this duty I
acquitted myself with distinction. A continental newspaper
remarked that I was a pioneer and had opened up new vistas
in music criticism. I am sure I did. But it was not entirely
my fault.

(2) During the 1948 Olympic Games I worked at Wembley

as a sports commentator with three of my Hungarian colleagues. At first I was a little shy, although we had been trained for the job with great care. On the second day of the Games, I was sitting next to one of the BBC's justly celebrated home-service commentators (who is no longer in this country) and, naturally, saw what he was seeing and heard what he was saying. His commentary gave me immense self-confidence. He knew still less about boxing than I did. Throughout the Olympic Games, we—my three colleagues and myself—gave a 2, 3 or 4 hours running commentary on all sorts of events. Millions were listening to us but I am sure not one listener noticed that music was really my strong point, while of sports I knew comparatively—I must stress the word *comparatively* —little.

(3) But my greatest achievement of all is that I never became a German monitor.

I should like to end this chapter by relating an incident in the Olymipc Games illustrating the dangers which lurk in wait for radio commentators and prophets in general. It is a story worth reflecting upon. It is a story with a moral for all of us.

There was an important boxing match between—let us say—an Austrian and a Persian. I was listening to the Austrian commentator who was sitting next to me in the broadcasting enclosure at Wembley Swimming Pool. He was extremely excited, his voice kept breaking, he was clearly suffering from great nervous strain, and talking at breath-taking speed. His commentary went something like this:

" This is wonderful . . . magnificent . . . The Persian champion—in spite of his truly amazing skill—just cannot stand up to our man. The Austrian boy is certainly on the top of his form. If he keeps this up, no-one will stand a chance with him, I can tell you that . . . He is landing one terrific punch after the other . . . a straight right . . . Another straight right . . . A smashing left to the stomach . . . He's fast, this Austrian boy, fast as lightning . . . Another straight right . . . The Persian cannot possibly stand this much

longer . . . He's weakening fast . . . I think he's exhausted . . .
He is staggering . . . This Austrian boy is simply
irresistible . . ."

Then a sudden break. A few minutes of inexplicable
silence followed. Then the announcer spoke again, in
lugubrious tone:

" The Austrian boy has just been knocked out."

PART III. *Literary*

ON MURDER

IN this part I should like to say a few words on the practical side of literature—or at least on that aspect of literary work in which I am interested. I shall start with the literature of murder but first, as a " lead-in," here are a few general observations on murder itself.

The English like murder. No other nation is so fond—indeed proud—of its murderers as the British.

Murder is an improper mode of behaviour but it seems to be a supreme entertainment. It costs far less lives than most other, apparently more orthodox, pastimes. Driving the family car for instance (what a touching picture it conjures up of Mum, Dad and the kiddies spending a lovely day together !) kills 4,000 people a year; the murderers account for about a hundred. Sport kills more people than murderers; drink kills more people; doctors kill more people; and poverty kills many more.

The English feel instinctively that many murderers are not really criminals. A pilferer or a petty thief is always a mean fellow; but murder is often committed by men of unimpeachable character and excellent reputation. Theft, forgery and income tax offences are always committed for material gain; murder is often committed out of tact and kindliness. Take a man for example who falls in love with a young woman but does not dare to tell his wife about it; he does not wish to hurt her feelings; he wishes to avoid vulgar quarrels; he does not want to leave her alone and uncared for in the world; he would hate to bring upon himself the scorn and censure of his neighbours, because people in England take a very poor view of a man who takes a solemn

oath at the age of twenty to love a woman forever and changes his mind thirty years later. So, to avoid a lot of unpleasantness, he kills his wife. If he is caught, he hangs and all is over in a few months; if he is undiscovered, he will have a full dose of the young beauty and in this way, very often, he meets his condign punishment.

I do not say that all murderers are nice people. There are all sorts in this world and naturally, you will find a number of unattractive characters even among murderers. But a murderer may be a nice fellow; a liar cannot be. Henry Cockburn—an Edinburgh barrister who played a part in the trial of William Burke in 1828 (and who was not Burke's counsel)—declared that apart from the murders he had committed, Burke was a very decent man. What he meant was this: if you glossed over the fact that Burke had killed sixteen people in order to sell their bodies to an anatomist for dissection (for £8–10 per *subject*), then, beneath this superficial layer of rough business methods, you found a likeable and jovial personality. It has been demonstrated that Burke was very fond of flowers and cats.

I personally also killed a man (See " Dybwad," in *Down with Everybody*! by the same author) although I am the kindest and noblest of men. It was an unfortunate necessity and I regret it. In principle I am against murder, and do not share the enthusiasm of the English public. But as De Quincey pointed out well over a hundred years ago, murder has not only a moral but also an aesthetic side. It can be, as indeed it often is, regarded as a work of art. It if is worth doing at all it is worth doing well. It is most regrettable that, as a rule, the death of an innocent person is involved. That is why old, historic murders and the fictitious murders of the detective novels are so popular in this country. You can gloat over them without hurting anybody's feelings. In detective novels the victim, more often than not, is a detestable person and consequently we are not prevented from giving our natural sympathies to the murderer; and of the victim, we can say that it served him right.

I must add that the laudable self-esteem and patriotism of the British tends to make them over-estimate their murderers. British murderers are capable, of course, and no country could be ashamed of them. They are often ingenious and origianl; they have often given a lead to the world; many of them were brave men and took incredible risks with admirable composure. But American murderers are more business-like, more matter of fact, more dramatic and work on a much larger scale. (About a hundred murders are committed in Britain in a year and about 7,000 in the United States.) Then the English almost always kill for money—an unpleasant, materialistic streak in their character—and the *crime passionel*, which gives such a romantic touch to many murders committed in France and other more hot-blooded countries, is almost completely lacking from our annals. But you will never persuade the English that their murderers are second to those of any other country. When some time ago the public executioner gave evidence before the Royal Commission on Capital Punishment, he made derogatory remarks about certain foreigners he had hanged and declared that the English took their punishment better than anyone else. At first sight, I thought this was patriotism far fetched; I felt it was wrong to boast that British murderers hanged better than foreigners. But I soon realised that it was the touchy foreigner at the bottom of my heart that was preventing me from seeing his point. Everybody judges human nature from his own angle; everybody studies people where he can see them. The executioner sees them most often under, or on, the gallows and why should he suppress his national pride in seeing that the English hang so much more co-operatively than aliens or naturalised British subjects ?

A lot has been written about the perfect crime, the writers always taking it for granted that the perfect crime is the undetected murder. This is silly. Murderers rarely wish to get away with it. They are extremely vain people and they love the limelight. They like to be tried and executed. It gives them a feeling of satisfaction. Murderers, after all, are

"Jolly good show, old man . . ."

even more popular than boxers and they know that one has to give one's whole life—in one way or another—to the pursuit of one's ambitions. When Burke—whom I have already mentioned—was awaiting execution in the condemned cell, only one thing bothered him. Dr. Knox, the anatomist, owed him £2 10s. for the last corpse he had delivered—the one that had proved Burke's downfall. His doom, however, had not cancelled the anatomist's debt to him and Burke energetically claimed the balance of £2 10s. because he wanted to buy a pair of shoes. He was to appear in public, he said (he was hanged publicly) and he insisted on wearing a decent pair of shoes on the day which he rightly regarded as the climax, almost the turning-point, of his career. A decent pair of shoes—that was the least, he felt, he owed his fans.

From the armchair detective's point of view the perfect crime may be the murder the perpetrator of which is never discovered; from the criminal's—or, if I may adopt De Quincey's terminology, from the artist's—point of view, it is the murder which is remembered and admired even after a century.

WHO DONE IT?

DETECTIVE novels are dangerous. They have never taught anybody to murder well; but they have taught many to write badly. I was already a grown-up man when I read the first specimen of the kind. Altogether I have read about eight or ten. I do not think I shall ever read another.

When I was a young man, I avoided detective novels for quite different reasons. My literary snobbishness prevented me from touching them. I walked about in Budapest carrying Proust very conspicuously under my arm, so that people should see what a highbrow I was. I think I should have died rather than be seen with a detective novel.

My snobbishness received its first heavy blow, and my whole literary outlook was infested with doubts, when I discovered that my father—my stepfather, to be quite precise—loved these novels. He was a much more cultured man than I could ever hope to be. I admired his encyclopaedic knowledge, his almost incredibly retentive memory, his thirst for almost any kind of information and his appreciation of scientific truth and artistic beauty. And then I discovered that he thrived on detective stories. He did not even deny it. He read them quite openly without the slightest feeling of shame. He is a doctor and I think one of the busiest doctors in Hungary. He worked (and still does) thirteen hours a day, from 8 a.m. until 9 p.m. six days a week. He has always been a slave, devoted to his duty, always at his patients' service. Nevertheless, my father once kept about twenty or more patients waiting for well over an hour while he finished some fearful rubbish (bound in canary yellow covers) rejoicing in the title of " X.Y.Z." I do not remember him ever doing such a thing before or since—for any reason whatever. Some time later, I also learned that one of my favourite authors—the last person I should have suspected—was addicted to detective

One of the busiest doctors

novels. I was shaken to my foundations; but I still would not touch the stuff.

When, years later, I bought my first green-bound pocket-edition, in England, I opened it with keen anticipation and with all the excitement of a small boy sneaking into the cinema to see and A-picture. I was full of expectation, even excitement. I deluded myself into thinking that I was about to enjoy forbidden fruit—and forbidden fruit is supposed to be so sweet. I was bored and disappointed—as one usually is by forbidden fruit.

I have read and listened to many arguments—some of them acrimonious—on the subject of whether detective fiction is good or bad literature. The answer is that it is neither good literature nor bad; it is not literature. I do not mean that it simply fails to reach the exalted heights of literature. No; it is not literature as smoked salmon is not literature. You may say that smoked salmon is better than literature; but you are bound to admit that it is different.

Would you call a stimulant or a sedative or a sleeping tablet *food*? You would not. Why not? You open your mouth, put the drug in, chew it and swallow it—in other words you treat it as you treat food. Still, this superficial resemblance does not mislead you in the case of food and drugs—you call food food and drugs drugs. You are not fooled as long as the drug is absorbed through your nutritive organs; you are, as soon as it is absorbed through your visual organs. Detective fiction is a drug consumed through the eyes.

It has nothing to do with literature. It is, I admit, slightly confusing that a detective novel *looks* like a book. This outward resemblance can be quite startling. A further source of confusion is that it is sold in bookshops and not at the chemist's. (Certain detective fiction, thrillers and ghost stories should be issued in the dispensing departments, on prescriptions only.) Furthermore, you go on deceiving yourself by putting the objects you have bought in the bookcase, instead of keeping them in the medicine cabinet along with the aspirins, sedatives and laxatives.

I think it is silly to speak of the " narrative power," " characterisation " and " style " of detective story writers, as they cannot have any. It is unfair to expect it from them. You do not expect narrative power from an aspirin tablet or grace of style from a bottle of laxative or a cross-word puzzle (another kind of drug masquerading in a semi-literary disguise). Let us be fair. And let us remember when reading a detective novel that it has nothing to do with literature. Reading this stuff you are smoking opium or marijuana; you are giving yourself an injection of morphia; you are having a glass of whisky or just smoking an ordinary cigar.

Whatever dazzling heights scientific progress may reach, in order to enjoy *War and Peace* you will always have to read it. But the time will soon come when detective novels can be injected subcutaneously by a syringe. Indeed, that time is here already. Another ten years of progress and you will be able to choose the author and the title for your injection.

AUTOBIOGRAPHY

SIR WINSTON CHURCHILL's autobiography should not mislead anyone. It is an old-fashioned work. You can never be quite sure whether he is writing the history of Europe or his own life-story. I cannot quite make up my mind whether in these volumes the history of the universe is disguised as Sir Winston's autobiography, or whether his autobiography is served up as the history of the universe. I have never accepted Sir Winston as a great statesman who is also a spare-time writer. Sir Winston—for me, at least—is first and foremost a writer and a spare-time statesman. Many writers have peculiar hobbies. One collects old waistcoats; another is passionately devoted to whist; Sir Winston Churchill spends his spare time in making world history. It is a legitimate pastime. From a strictly professional point of view, however, it is his own, private concern.

During the war, I looked forward to its end for many reasons, one being that I wanted to see what Sir Winston would make of it as a writer. Now that I have read the volumes hitherto published, I am bitterly disappointed. I liked his earlier works—historical or otherwise—incomparably more. In *The Second World War* the statesman has got the better of the writer. It is not a writer's book like *The World Crisis*, for instance; it is the Prime Minister's book. During the last war Sir Winston had a fairly good observation point; yet, his book is not the observer's book. Instead of describing and discussing past events, he is arguing a case. And his example should serve as a strong warning to beginners: private hobbies are all right as long as they do not interfere with, or influence, your literary activities. Your private war is one thing; but the book you write about it for a large public is quite another.

But as I have already said, Churchill's memoirs are not

Spare-time statesman

typical. He wages modern wars but writes old-fashioned books about them.

If I ever come to write my own autobiography, I shall have to decide which of the two leading patterns to follow. Shall I deify or lousify myself ? " Am I Napoleon . . . or am I a louse ?"—exclaimed that celebrated neurotic of world literature, Raskolnikov. Napoleon or a louse ? It is obvious that people dislike being anything between the two. If you follow Pattern No. 1, you must write in a modest tone and be satisfied to paint yourself as Napoleon. Following Pattern No. 2, you can be much more pretentious.

Pattern No. 1 is fashionable in England today. In the preface, you are expected to explain that you never thought of writing you autobiography. What, a whole book on yourself ? Why should you ? Who are you, after all ? Only a former Viceroy of India or the chairman of a tyre-manufacturing firm, lately elevated to the peerage. You would not have dreamt of writing a book on your life but for the insistent clamour of your admirers. (If you want to be disarmingly modest, use the phrase " millions of admirers," to show that the utmost pressure was needed to persuade you.) Then you sit down, write the book and call it *A story Not Worth Telling* (12 Volumes) ; or : *Notes on an Unimportant Life* (3 Volumes with 72 photographs of the author) ; or : *I Have Nothing to Say* . . .) (2,143 pages, 3 guineas).

These works are always modest and clean, having nothing in common with such immoral books as the autobiographies of Stendhal or Proust. Sex is out ; immoral thoughts are out ; religious doubts are out ; discussions on problems of a patriotic nature are out ; even party-political convictions are taken for granted and inherited from your father. Intellectual and spiritual worries are not simply avoided : they just do not exist. Matters of fact are related in every detail without any reference to motive.

In Pattern No. 2, you dwell on motives and do not bother about facts. You have to revel in dirt and to make yourself interesting. You spit in your own face twice on every page.

You admit that it was your design to commit all the basest crimes in the world. You confess, for example, that when you arrived home one day as a youth and asked your elder sister for a piece of bread and butter and marmalade, it was really because you were looking for a way to start an immoral relationship with her. All that actually did happen, of course, was that you asked for a piece of bread and butter and marmalade, you got it, thanked her most politely, whereupon she went back to her room to mend her stockings. Who could have imagined the whirlwinds of emotions, tornados of passions and tragedies of repressed lust behind a simple scene like that? Once again, when your father refused to give you two and ninepence to go to Highbury, you wanted to kill him. To stab him with a daggar! Your own father! For a small sum like that—the price of the cheapest ticket (inclusive of entertainment tax). It is true that answering him you only said: "All right, Daddy, maybe I can go next week." A simple, almost touching little family scene—but what sinister shadows and Freudian tension behind it. And so on you go, describing your life which consists of going to the office at 9 a.m., returning at 5.30 p.m., having lunch at a cafeteria on weekdays and taking long walks with your mother-in-law on Sunday afternoons. These are the outward events of your life; but you bring in your thoughts, your insistent, self-analysis, and you transform this mild, domestic tale into a tragedy of self-torture, crime, lechery, sadism, attempted murder and incest. You bare your soul and lay it on thick. " ' No more marmalade, Jocelyn,' I groaned, and looked at her neck with glassy eyes. ' No more marmalade ' .... Oh, if she only knew ... if she only knew ... "

We have to choose between Pattern No. 1 and No. 2. Both patterns have given a few masterpieces to the world. Both are workable—it is really a matter of taste which you choose. One prefers swaggering this way, another that way.

Choose your pattern and remember three final important rules.

(1) Whatever you write—a novel, an historical essay or

a mathematical treatise—you are always writing about yourself, giving away involuntarily, as it were, some of your innermost secrets. An essay on indirect taxation may be as self-revealing as lyric poetry. Autobiography is the only exception: very often it tells us little or nothing of its author. So, as a literary form, it may be recommended to the shy and diffident.

(2) Do not bother about getting your facts right. You cannot possibly remember them and you will mix them up in any case. I have never seen an autobiography in which even the basic facts and data were correct.

(3) Do not try to be objective. The whole charm and appeal of an autobiography is its bias, its personal and egotitsic angle. Tell about your likes and dislikes, lash out at your enemies and pose as an archangel if you can do so with an air of modesty. You have lost battles in the field but you can refight and win them on paper. Or at least blame others for the defeats. To say: " I lost the battles because the others were stronger and more intelligent and better led,"—is just not playing the game of autobiography. The stain of objectivity spoils an autobiography just as a plea of " guilty " spoils a promising murder trial. Do not hand yourself; give others a chance.

NOVEL

IF you write a novel, your manuscript will be weighed before it is read. Weighed—not in any metaphorical sense. It will be weighed on scales and if it is found wanting—that is, shorter than 75,000 words—it will not be read at all. Should it be abnormally long it will not be considered, either. Why? Because the lending libraries will not buy novels which are too short. The borrower reads them much too quickly and returns to worry the librarian for another book; nor will the libraries buy an abnormally long book for the simple reason that it costs too much. Sociologists and literary historians keep writing learned tracts on the various influences which form and shape the modern novel. Their speculation is usually as exciting and instructive as it is wide of the mark. The greatest single influence on the 20th-century English novel is the lending library. From the publisher's point of view the lending library is the buying library. The libraries have so many customers who consume so much printed material per week. It is a question of steady and easily calculable supply and demand, just like the fish-market.

The fish-market—with some differences:

(1) An average 20th-century fish is of higher literary merit than the average 20th-centry novel.

(2) If the fish is too small or too big, it can be chopped up, its trunk sold to one customer and its tail to another. Libraries, of course, could do the same with novels. There are many people who only read the beginning of a novel and then stop; others only read the end because by reading the end they can guess the beginning. Still, fiction-mongers do not chop, bone, skin and fillet books. Not yet, anyway. We must not blame them for this. This is no discourtesy to the public or lack of desire to serve us properly. On reflection, we must admit that fish-mongers, too, might be compelled to change their whole practice if they were only lending fish and not selling it.

But there we are. Emily Bronté had enough difficulty in finding a publisher; today she would fail completely. *Wuthering Heights* is not quite 75,000 words long. *Nicholas Nickleby*—if written by an unknown author—would not be published today. It is too long. Nor would *A Christmas Carol* appear. It is too short. But, of course, the young Dickens, aspiring to be a novelist, would never write them. He would know better. He would comply with the wishes of the lending libraries and publishers. Because an artist cannot work without inspiration. The best and most effective inspiration is a cheque in advance. And in the last twenty-five years the lending libraries have had a hand in all literary and poetic inspiration.

A good novel is a great achievement. It can shatter, amuse, purify and change you. But a good novel is as rare as a good historical essay on 9th-century church history. The failure of the novelist is only more conspicuous because so many more people try to write novels than essays on 9th-century church history. I believe it is more difficult to write a good novel than to write almost anything else good, including even a good play.

If you sit down to write a novel, you must be a " born story-teller." To have a " shrewd knowledge of human nature" used to suffice, but it is no longer enough. As a born story-teller, you must rely on your story. Many a reader's only interest is: *what next* ? The more unexpected and unlikely it is, the better. " Story" in England and America means violence. English novelists kill many more—incomparably more—people than English murderers; and *Variety* has reported that an average of 46 people are being killed every week on American sound radio programmes alone. I have in front of me Mr. Somerset Maugham's short stories—over a hundred stories in three volumes. Mr. Maugham is certainly a born sotry-teller and knows his public. About two-thirds of his stories consist of murder, suicide and other violence—but mostly murder. And, if I made a thorough survey of modern English and American novels—the result, I fear, would be similar.

My first objection to this massacre carried out by our novelists is that it is unrealistic. Not everybody is a murderer. I have known many people who never killed anybody. I myself have killed one man only, but the whole incident is hardly worth mentioning. I have been living in a large block of flats for over ten years now and, so far as I know, there has not been a single murder in the block. There may have been minor murders of small public interest but I have heard of none. People, it is true, are in the habit of dying. Some die at the end of their lives, some in the middle and others at the beginning. Novelists, describing life, must also describe death. But not all deaths are murder. This is an important point, largely forgotten in Britain and America. People are not really in the habit of being murdered. The Average Man, the Little Man, the Common Man (whose century ours is sometimes ironically called) is more often not murdered than otherwise. The Man in the Dark Shed may be murdered; The Man in the Street is not. I admit that life would be more interesting and eventful if more murders were committed. Novelists are, to a certain extent, entitled to encourage practitioners of murder to be more active. But, after all, their (the novelists') duty is to picture life as it is and not as it ought to be.

My second main objection is—and this is purely personal —that all these murders bore me stiff. Muder in life and literature is a cowardly evasion; it is dodging the real problems. Human passion, jealousy, love, avarice and all the various obsessions are mysterious, unfathomable and of permanent interest: violence is dull. Suppose the hero of your novel needs £137 10s. 3d. cash. The reader is thrilled and excited because, as it happens, he too, needs exactly the same amount and a little more. Indeed, one of the basic problems of the fifties is, how to get £137 10s. 3d. cash and a little more. One is full of expectation to see how a literary master is going to solve this great problem. Then your hero goes and kills an old garage proprietor who has the money. What an anticlimax! How flat!

If you want to become a modern novelist, you must decide what kind of people you are going to write about. The

Hardly worth mentioning

early Victorians painted on a vast canvas, and dealt with masses of people—old and young, rich and poor, people of all trades and all walks of life. Today, we live in an age of specialists and experts. Novelists depict a small section of life and tell us about a short period or some few episodes of certain people's lives. Some novelists only write of aircraft-designers, others of neurotics and psychopaths; others deal exclusively with the landed gentry or what is left of them, others with journalists and again others with retired senior civil servants or American gangsters settled in London. It has been suggested that patents should be issued to novelists, so that one writer should not encroach on another's field. Chartered accountants are still free, and also Chelsea pensioners and dustmen. I believe that is all.

Your other preoccupation, if you wish to follow the fashion, should be love. All novelists write in our dreary, poor, unromantic, worry-ridden, prosaic and petty-minded world as if it were full of Romeos concerned only and exclusively with their respective Juliets, and vice versa. At the same time, sex is still taboo in English novels. Perhaps not an absolute taboo since the stork story has been definitely given up.

Mr. Terrence Rattigan has written a play dealing with the beautiful and poetic subject of a woman's love. Love is the whole world for the heroine, while for the hero it is something quite pleasant but utterly unimportant. In the words of one of the critics: " To him—a former test pilot—it is something that must take its place along with golf and pub-crawling and many other innocent diversions." This is the individual problem of all modern novelists. They write as if love were our whole life, while to the normal majority it takes its place along with other more or less innocent interests. But most of our novelists have not noticed this; or they write for a public which refuses to accept realities; or they deliberately paint a false picture to fool themselves. Romantic love—as then pictured—simply did not exist in the age of mediaeval knights; and does not exist today.

A few days ago someone remarked to me—trying to express agreement with me on this subject—that he did not believe in the suburban fire damage assessor who is supposed to be suffering like any hero of Balzac's because his ageing wife has eloped with a rope merchant. He might be annoyed, my friend added, but he is probably more preoccupied in jotting down little figures on the margin of *The Financial Times*. It is likely that he hates telling his story in the office and the club but he does not really care; indeed, after a few days he has a good and hearty laugh at the expense of the rope merchant. The case as my friend put it, is probably largely true but I fail to see what the whole affair has to do with the man's occupation. Has a fire damage assessor a funny profession ? Is there any such thing as a funny profession at all ? Why should a fire damage assessor's feelings differ from the feelings of an actor, a diplomatist or an electrician ? But the picture drawn by my friend is, I believe, true, in the case of all of them, excepting of course those people who are the permanent or temporary spiritual relations of Mr. Rattigan's hero.

I think if you wish to be a truthful novelist of a coming age, you must accept a new reality. Our age is not a wicked age—as some writers try to portray it; it is not a terrified age; it is not a romantic age; it is not an immoral age; it is not the Age of Longing; it is not the Age of Anxiety. It is the Age of Emptiness. Ours is a world swept away from its moorings and drifting nowhere in particular. What can one say about this? Nothing. And our novelists say it. Not very well, but they say it.

IF you want to get reviews, you must become news. This is the safest way. A new volume of Sir Winston Churchill's memoirs is discussed by all the papers in leading articles. It is very useful for an author to be Prime Minister of the land at the same time. It gives you a lot of publicity and helps to smooth matters in general.

If you cannot (or do not want to) become Prime Minister you may still be news. A new book by Mr. Graham Greene (but only since his becoming a great success as a screen writer) is news; should Woodcock, the boxer, publish his autobiography, that would also be news; if the 237th former Minister or Gauleiter issues his reminiscences, proving that he worked for the Allies during the war and founded the German resistance movement, that is again news.

Further tips about getting publicity.

(1) Be a peer. If you are a duke, your sales may reach astonomical figures. But almost anything down to a baronetcy will help.

(2) Get into scandals. Beat your wife publicly. Elope with the daughter of some very respectable father. Kill someone. Marry a film-star. If you cannot do better, drive under the influence of drink. The last is a poor show but better than nothing.

(3) Pornography, too, is always a safe bet in this puritanical land. A menacing and damning question in the House of Commons is worth more than scores of laudatory reviews, each of them a column long. No praise can really match the value of a devastating attack.

If you are not inclined to follow these lines—some authors are still unduly shy and hesitant—you have to take your place in the queue. Papers may—or may not—review your work, it depends on a great many things. But does it really matter ? Sometimes it does, sometimes it does not. There is one paper which sells 7 million copies and is read presumably by 20 or 25 millions. Half of the nation. But I am sure it is that half of the nation which hardly ever touches a book. So what does it matter if that paper praises or condemns you—provided, of course, that it reviews books at all which I doubt very much and am not going to find out. Then, funnily enough, I have never met one single person who listened to a book review on the air, except the author, his wife and his mother, the reviewer's wife and *his* mother. I know that there must be up to 15 million people who do listen in; but I seem to meet the other 30 million.

Reviews written for readers—and it does not matter whether these *readers* are buyers or borrowers of books—are much more interesting, no matter what their circulation is. Some reviews induce people to read a book; and some books even induce a reviewer to read the book in question. It does not occur very often but I have on several occasions had the feeling that the reviewer had actually read my book or seen it from quite close quarters.

People have little space today and the paper shortage has made a great impression on the art of criticism. 58 novels are lumped together in one short review and the reviewer says things like " more impish than thorough . . . " . . . " lit up by dramatic scenes " . . . " romantic but readable " . . . " quite readable but unromantic " . . . " makes interesting reading . . . " . . . " the story has significance and delicacy . . ." . . . " the story has delicacy, but lacks significance . . . " . . . " it is fragmentary but well informed " . . . Probably all this has some meaning. I often try to imagine the reader— eager to get some information on new books—reading such a review and exlcaiming with joy: " Oh . . . more impish than thorough ! The very thing I'm after. I've been looking for years for a book more impish than thorough. But my unfortunate lot has been to read books which were more thorough than impish. Now, at last, my chance has come." —And he shoots off to the nearest bookshop.

Of course, not all authors are lucky enough to be treated

to such deep, brilliant and anlytical reviews as these. (And not all readers get such valuable information.) Some must be satisfied with " Reviews in Brief." Such as: " L. Tolstoy: Wr & Pce. Too lng bt extrmly readbl. F. Dostoevsky: Cr. & Pun. A non-Commun. Russian. Almost a 2nd Ag. Christie. Recomm. T. Branwell: The Silver Key. Extng. Brllnt. Mr imp thn thrgh."

Still, there are certain critics who are given a comparatively huge amount of space in the various literary organs. They can afford to give a full and longish article to one single book. In order to be noticed by them it is advisable:

(1) To deal with a minor, forgotten, unread literary curiosity.

(2) who is preferably dead for at least eighty years.

Write a long, tedious and well documented critical biography of Thomas Otway and, although no-one is likely to read it, most of the star critics of our press will hail it with breathless excitement as if a new era had opened in English literature. They will not have the public believe that they do not know anything about Thomas Otway; that they are not familiar with every line Thomas Otway wrote. They will correct minor biographical details. They will rejoice in this and have the pleasant feeling that they are talking above the heads of ordinary mortals. And a number of ordinary mortals, reading this highly distinguished balderdash, will also have the feeling of being lifted on to a higher spiritual plane. Many of these star-critics are the products of the Literary Editor's guilt complex. He has made too many concessions to the trashy and popular; he must make some concessions to the snobs, as well. Blessed be the memory of Thomas Otway ! It is all very fair: there will be a time when all present-day writers will have been dead for 80 years. So why complain ?

Advertisement is another great problem for the author. Authors always think that the publisher has spent too little on advertisements; publishers are always convinced that they have spent too much. The argument goes on. But both publishers and authors are working under a misconception.

It is not the author who sould be advertised; it is the reader.

I heard once about a family in a little Surrey town. It belonged to what is termed in this country the lower middle class. They wanted to buy either a television set or a piano for the daughter of the house, and they could not make up their minds which. It was no easy decision. The daughter herself kept a lady-friend of mine informed of the wavering and swaying of the family council. At last—my friend was informed—the family had made a decision: " We are going to buy the piano for me," said the daughter. My lady-friend congratulated her. The girl herself, however, did not appear too happy about the arrangement. " There is only one thing . . . " she said, and hesitated. " Yes, we wonder," she said at last, "whether we could not put something up on the roof to show we have a piano." This was very sincere and sensible. It made another friend of mine meditate on these problems and he made a wonderful invention: television antennæ without the sets. He is going to form a company and sell them by the million. Such an antennae will cost a trifle and look exactly like the real one. It will in fact be the real antenna.

I wonder whether we could not follow this lead ? Could we not arrange for something to be put on the roof showing that the occupier of the house is reading a book ? If we could advertise the reader and his cultural activities instead of the author and his book, I am sure we could create a new and undreamed-of boom in the publishing trade.

Someone reading

YOU must beware of writing a best-seller. One cannot be too careful. If you are not on your guard, you may be landed with a great success before you notice it. Many reckless people have brought immense trouble on themselves, thanks to their own foolishness.

" What is wrong with best-sellers ?" the uninitiated reader may ask.

I have already discussed the moral stigma it brings upon you. Your colleagues who bring out their learned, critical treatises on Thomas Otway and are applauded, hailed and extolled by the One Man One Book critics, despise and condemn you. It is not envy they feel; it is sheer disgust. Could you bear this ? Would you consider life worth living if the authors of the Thomas Otway tradition frowned upon you ?

But the moral stigma—aggravating as it is—is not all. A best-seller brings in its wake innumerable financial worries as well. I have written a best-seller, to be sure, on a very modest scale—nothing to compare with an American or even the record type of English best-seller—and yet, it caused me tremendous financial troubles. "What can you do with all that money ?" people often ask me. If they only knew what a sore point they are touching, they would never ask that question. Yes, my greatest worry has been, for a long time now, what to do with all that money. Money keeps pouring in relentlessly; you are on the brink of despair; but you cannot stem the flood. You hardly dare to open your letters, lest you find more and more cheques in them and your worst fears prove constantly justified. You may bewail your fate; you may feel like imploring mercy. But once you have taken the fatal step, there is no mercy for you. I am at my wit's end, but I just do not know how to get rid of all that money. After all, you cannot buy more than two dozen mink coats

Imploring for mercy . . . .

for your wife; after all, it looks like showing off it you keep
driving about the town in six Rolls Royces at once. (Driving
one and having five on tow, I mean.) Occasionally in my
despair I am driven to going down the street to distribute
five-pound notes among the passers-by. But that, of course,
is no easy way out of the mess I landed myself in. You know
how reserved English people are. They do not accept your
money in the street; they shake their heads and go on with a
contemptuous smile on their lips—just because we have not
been properly introduced to one another.

But there is an even more serious worry connected with
best-sellers. People identify you with them and whatever you
do, whatever else you may write, you remain just the author of
that one single book. "Yes, it's not bad," people will say of
your latest effort, " but it is not another *How to be an Alien.*"
Mr. Somerset Maugham has complained about this bitterly and
repeatedly. Whatever he did, he was told that he would never
create another *Of Human Bondage.* Recently I read Robert
Graves' latest book, *Occupation Writer.* He quotes an
imaginary bookseller talking about him: " Pity he couldn't
have given us another *I Claudis* instead . . . "

These two writers may be much more eminent than I am;
but the problem is the same. You, as an author, have the
justified or unjustified impression that you have learnt
something; that you have matured; that you have more to
say than you had before and that you say it better. And then
people come and rub your first success in—trying to make it
out to be your last. The terrifying thought is always there, of
course: they may be right. Has Maugham really ever
surpassed *Of Human Bondage* ? Has Graves ever written
anything more brilliant than the Claudius books? Have I
really . . . Yes, of course, I have.

You do not want to be disloyal to your past. You do not
wish to deny your earlier works: they are a part of you. But
you refuse to stand in front of the world in ridiculously
outgrown childish clothes. If you reach a certain age, and a
certain girth, you do not feel comfortable riding a tricycle

wearing short trousers with mittens on your hands, a large pink ribbon in your hair and a bib round your neck. You have to choose, like all writers: you either go on babbling and using baby talk all your life (as many do), or else you will be charged with having lost your girlish laughter and your puerile charm. And it is so true: we all were so much sweeter when we were three.